BARTENDING 101

THE BASICS OF MIXOLOGY

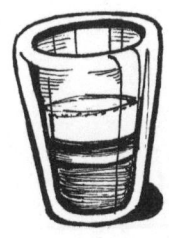

FOURTH EDITION

HARVARD STUDENT AGENCIES, INC.
BARTENDING COURSE

ANN LAI, EDITOR

ILLUSTRATED BY DIANA SAVILLE

Bartending 101: The Basics of Mixology, Fourth Edition. Copyright © 2005 by Harvard Student Agencies, Inc. All rights reserved. Printed in the United States of America. No part of this book may be used or reproduced in any manner whatsoever without written permission except in the case of brief quotations embodied in critical articles or reviews. For information, address St. Martin's Press, 175 Fifth Avenue, New York, NY 10010.

www.stmartins.com
www.harvardstudentagencies.com/hbc/

Design: Ann Lai

ISBN 0-312-34906-8
EAN 978-0-312-34906-6
Fourth St. Martin's Edition: November 2005.

10 9 8 7 6 5 4 3 2 1

BARTENDING 101

THE BASICS OF MIXOLOGY

CONTENTS

HARVARD STUDENT AGENCIES
CALEB MERKL, PRESIDENT
ROBERT ROMBAUER, GENERAL MANAGER

SPECIAL THANKS TO
ANNE CHISHOLM
NAHU GHEBREMICHAEL
STUART ROBINSON
AUSTIN BLACKMON
MICHELLE WHITE
KIM HOLMES
TOM MERCER

This book is based on the course by Adam J. Tocci. Without his extensive work the course, and the book, would not exist.

INTRODUCTION

It took thousands, nay, millions of years for humankind to evolve to the point where its opposable thumbs allowed the species to finally achieve success in its tumultuous struggle to twist open a beer. And when this great triumph was achieved, there was much rejoicing, and much consumption of said beer... which might explain why the early clans of nomadic drinkers spent much time in their caves, hiding from the pounding sunlight, quivering in their intoxicated and subsequent hungover states. And in this darkness, it proved difficult for further evolution to transpire, for it was extremely difficult to successfully mix a drink in the absence of light. But then the noble clan of the bartenders emerged, and ushered in a new age of enlightenment and wisdom, vanquishing the beasts of ignorance with the bald proclamation, "A dry martini shall mix but a small dash of vermouth with a much, much larger quantity of gin." And thus was born a new era, in which witticisms uttered from the sacred throne known as a bar stool became an acceptable substitute for work and productivity. And so did humankind demonstrate its gratitude by showering upon the bartender many tips and great affection, thereby making membership in the noble clan of bartenders appealing to all.

Because bartenders still occupy a much ballyhooed position in society, many people continue to seek the grail that is a Masters of Mixology. For too long, this quest has seemed distant and even impossible, a ream deferred for the easily dissuaded. This book, however, seeks to overcome that difficulty by demonstrating that the basics of bartending are easily learned. At a fundamental level, there is nothing complicated about bartending—the most crucial components are patience, practice, and persistence. Style and flair come with time, but bartending jobs and brilliantly orchestrated parties emerge out of a set of sound fundamentals that guide in the expert production of tasty beverages.

For twenty-five years now, the Harvard Student Agencies Bartending Course has been turning amateur bartenders into an elite force of talented mixologists, spreading joy and well-prepared drinks throughout the world. Now, the accumulated wisdom of these decades squeezes itself into this book in hopes that you, dear reader, can enjoy the noble pursuit of the properly prepared drink and use it as a force for good, whether throwing the most brilliant of private parties or satisfying the most demanding patron at some watering hole. Along these lines, it bears mentioning that the techniques outlined in this book can serve as a point of departure into professional bartending, which is an excellent source of part-time jobs and spending money for college students, or fulltime work with fine pay in an extremely satisfying and very interactive line of duty.

At its core, bartending is a simple art, and this book is designed to show you the ropes as quickly and efficiently as possible. In Chapter One, you'll learn the basics about the organization of a bar, and the not so basics about the characters of all of the liquid actors in the pageant of drinks. Chapter Two offers the supporting cast, detailing the technology and complementary flavors with which a bartender regularly works. Chapter Three examines the processes and recipes necessary to produce the most popular categories of mixed drinks. Chapters Four and Five counter with the oft-overlooked world of beer and wine. Chapter Six includes a discussion of some innovative uses for beer, wine, and champagne. More unorthodox categories of drinks emerge in Chapter Seven, offering some unusual and memorable varieties that will make a fantastic impression at any party; additionally, the chapter offers an arsenal of non-alcoholic drinks that is a crucial component of the good bartender's repertoire. Chapter Eight offers some helpful hints to make sure that your private soirees run smoothly. Chapter Nine follows by examining how to make the jump into the professional ranks of bartenders. Finally, Chapter Ten offers some cautionary advice on alcohol's side effects and the responsibilities of the bartender.

CHAPTER 1:
LIQUID TOOLS

The contents of liquor bottles often seem like the magical arsenal of a witch's brew. Confusion abounds among bartenders as to what, exactly, they're dumping into their delicious concoctions. Knowledge is power, however, and a basic sense of the subtle flavors that comprise a tasty mixed beverage can help to turn a babe in the bartending woods (it is, of course, illegal to hire infants as mixologists) into a certified escort in the world of liquid delectation. This chapter seeks to enable that transition, first by examining the basic setup of a bar and its correspondence to frequently ordered drinks, then by providing a sketch of the manifold flavors that comprise the masterful bartender's creative palette.

BASIC BAR SETUP

If you've ever looked closely at a professional bar or someone's well-stocked home bar, you've probably noticed that bottles are generally kept in two main areas: the "front bar" and the "back bar." A good bottle arrangement enables bartenders to make drinks efficiently, without having to search all over the place for the bottle that they need.

At the front bar, also known as the "well" or the "cocktail party bar," bartenders mix more than 70% of their drinks. As these names suggest, all the basic, most popular drinks can be made using the bottles located in this area.

A typical front bar setup is shown on pages 8 and 9. Vodka, gin, rum, tequila, and triple sec, from right to left – the light alcohols – go on your right. If you're serving drinks to a young crowd, you'll find that light alcohols are more popular than dark and should be placed according to your handedness: on the right for right-handed people and on the left for southpaws. This arrangement allows for slightly greater speed, which is a crucial component in bartending. On your left, from right to left, are whiskey, bourbon, Scotch, Rose's Lime Juice, and grenadine – the dark alcohols plus a couple of frequently used mixers. In the middle rest dry vermouth and sweet vermouth. The row of fancy bottles represents the "show row," which is found on some professional and large home bars. It is exactly the same as those behind it, except that each remains sealed and has the label facing the guests so that they can see which brands the bartender is pouring. The show row really doesn't have an official function other than to inform guests what is being served, and it is often omitted.

This setup, while common, is not absolute. Depending on the alcohol preferences of your guests, it is generally safe to say that the best setup involves placing the bottles that will be used with the most frequency within easy reach while not interrupting the normal order of the speed rail. For instance, add a bottle of coffee brandy to the end of the well on May Day when a bunch of Commies will flood the bar begging for White Russians.

While there are occasionally variations on the basic ordering principle of the well, such anomalies are not frequent. Try to learn to work with the diagrammed order, but if you find yourself working in an establishment that follows different organizational principles, make sure that you learn them immediately – disrupting someone's setup can lead to disastrous outcomes, and a lot of very unpleasant drinks. The purpose of organizational consistency is to increase the efficiency with which you can serve drinks by placing the bottles in the same place every time so that you can grab them blindly.

In professional bars, a "speed rail" usually replaces the front bar. This rack, attached to the bar or sink directly in front of the bartender, holds "house brands" (usually less-expensive brands) of front-bar liquor. The bartender defers to the well brand of liquor for every drink unless the customer specifies a well-known brand, or "call brand," as it is known in bartending lingo. The more expensive call brands stay on the back bar. That means that you will prepare a White Russian with generic coffee brandy instead of the most commonly known call brand (Kahlúa) unless the drinker specifically requests otherwise (or if your bar is using Kahlúa as its well brand). There is a further classification of alcohols called the "premium" or "top-shelf" brands. These are even higher quality bottles of liquor – such as Bombay gin or Old Grand Dad bourbon

YOUR BASIC BAR SETUP

You may have read all about these things just a brief moment ago in the text, but this will remind you of what you've already read! It will also help visual learners catch up to all those textual learners for whom these whole two pages are probably just incomprehensible squiggles and nonsense.

SHOW BOTTLES

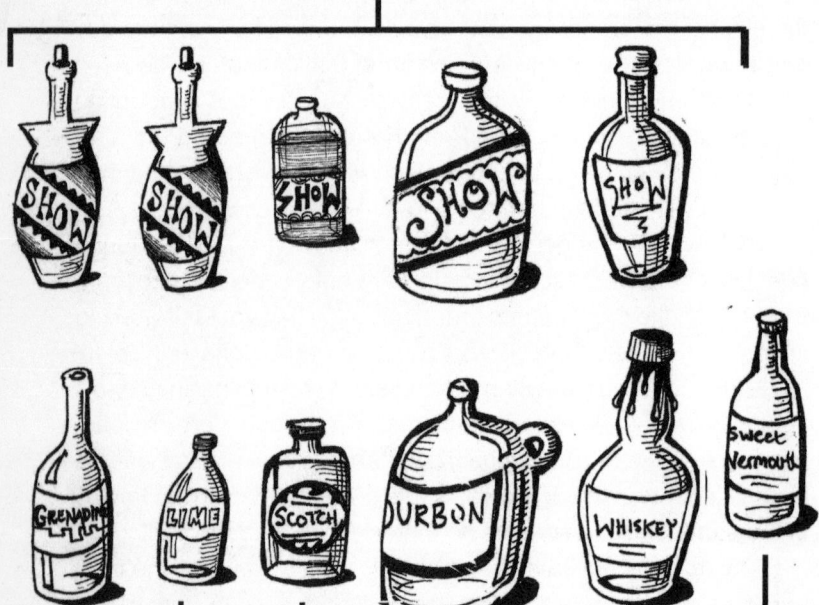

Lime Juice
Always use Rose's Lime juice. Why? People deserve only the best in lime juice.

Grenadine
Sweet and delicious! Often used for Shirley Temples and Roy Rogerses.

Scotch
Like blended whiskey, except grosser.

Bourbon
Bourbon is perhaps the most delicious of the dark alcohols – a Maker's Mark and water will always hit the spot, no matter what the occasion or hour of the morning.

Whiskey
Do keep the blended whiskey in the well, because it is the whiskey that tastes worst.

Sweet Vermouth
If you get the opportunity, you should see Makavajev's *Sweet Movie*. It will blow your mind. Sweet vermouth is used for martinis.

Bartender
If this two-page spread were an actual bar setup, you would find yourself somewhere in the middle of the binding.

THE SHOW BOTTLES: Use these in fancy bars to show the customers what they're getting. Do not use in unfancy bars. Theoretically, they are the same brand as the one that's actually in your well, but this drawing is theoretically not theory-based.

Dark Vermouth
Used for the most masculine of drinks, the Manhattan.

Tequila
Why is there a market today for high class tequilas? You might as well quaff a $1000 bottle of vintage grappa and drink your own urine.

Gin
Consistently the booze with the shortest, classiest name. Close finishers: rum.

Triple Sec
A new addition to the modern 'tender's well. As it turns out, people like the way it tastes. Who doesn't love a good sidecar?

Rum
The misunderstood booze with a Caribbean flair.

Vodka
Here's an example of a good vodka: Ketel One. Here's an example of what you keep in the well: Cossack's White Devil.

– that cost even more than their counterparts, These bottles will also find a home on the back bar. There will generally be a list in the bars designating a price for each individual brand of alcohol.

The back bar, also called the "liqueur bar," contains liqueurs, brandies, and other less frequently ordered liquors. As the name suggests, bartenders usually keep those bottles behind them, since they rarely have to use these liquors and don't mind walking a few extra steps when they need them.

At first glance, the back bar appears to be a confusing array of bottles, apparently thrown onto the shelves in random order. Actually, the organization of the back bar follows two basic and sensible rules:

RULE 1: Keep bottles on the back bar separated by flavor base. For example, put the four orange-flavored liqueurs together, the Kahlúa next to the coffee-flavored brandy, and all the call brands of Scotch near each other.

RULE 2: Keep bottles used for the same drink together whenever possible. For example, keep the brandy next to the crème de menthe so that you can quickly grab both of them to make a stinger. Chapter 3 will give you an idea of the more common liquor combinations.

MIXERS

Bartenders usually keep at least four carbonated mixers on the front bar. **COLA** and **TONIC WATER** go best with light alcohols (as in rum and Coke or gin and tonic). Soda and ginger ale mix well with dark alcohols (as in Scotch and soda or bourbon and ginger). You might also want to have other carbonated mixers at the bar, such as **7-UP** or **SPRITE**, **BITTER LEMON**, **SOUR MIX**, or any other of the many mixers available. Don't forget diet sodas; many people try to convince themselves that their drinks don't have that many calories by requesting diet sodas as mixers.

Bottled mixers will suffice for the home bar or for a small, relaxed corner pub; soda taps work well in medium-sized, moderately busy bars; but when dealing with large, crowded, high-pressure establishments, only a "soda gun" keeps the mixer flowing fast enough. Also known as an "arm" or a "snake," this dispenser consists of a long, flexible tube with a set of buttons on the end. Each button represents a mixer; the bartender merely pushes a button, and the desired soda gushes out of the gun. This device eliminates the inefficient hassle of searching all over the place for bottles, uncapping them, and running out every two minutes. If you work in a bar with a snake, ask the manager or a co-worker to show you how to set it up and make minor repairs.

It's important to remember that there is a big difference between tonic water and soda water. **SODA WATER** (generally identified by an "S" on the soda gun) is merely carbonated water – in its own right, it is flavorless, but it has some hyperactive carbon dioxide kicking around to give it "texture." **TONIC WATER** (generally noted with a "Q" on the soda gun, short for quinine, an ingredient in tonic water) on the other hand, is carbonated, flavored water, generally resembling a slightly bitter lemon or lime taste that is softened by a small amount sugar and all of its friendly bubbles. If you aren't using a soda gun, you can distinguish between the two waters by their labels – soda water has a blue label, while tonic water has a yellow label.

JUICES, of course, also go well with many liquors. Some popular mixing juices are orange, grapefruit, pineapple, cranberry, and tomato. There is no set order for how juices are kept at a bar, although it is important to know that they are kept in "juicers," instead of in clumsy cartons. Juicers are just containers with twist off tops that have attachable nozzles. They are referred to in the trade as "store and pours," since the speedpourer allows for easy pourin' of drinks, while the covers allow the juice to be stored overnight so that it doesn't turn rancid. Juices don't have a set order at the bar – you'll just have to identify the various beverages by their color (easily done for tomato and orange juices, but to distinguish between pineapple and grapefruit juice, you'll probably have to open up the juicer and sniff to clarify which is which).

Many drinks such as Collinses, sours, and daiquiris, call for **SOUR MIX**. This mixer contains lemon juice, sugar, and sometimes egg white to make the drink slightly foamy. Sour mix often comes in powdered form (Quik-Lem for example); in a pinch you can substitute frozen lemonade mixed with half the prescribed water.

OTHER MIXERS INCLUDE:

ROSE'S LIME JUICE: A reconstituted lime juice used most often in gimlets. Rose's is sweetened, so do not substitute it in recipes calling for plain lime juice.

CREAM: Don't use anything heavier than light cream or half-and-half, or you'll fill the drinker's stomach too quickly.

MILK: For Sombreros, especially. It can be used as a substitute for cream.

WATER: To mix with whiskey. If your bar does not dispense water through a tap or a snake, keep water in a pitcher so that all the air will dissipate. Otherwise, drinks will appear cloudy from tiny air bubbles in the tap water.

ALCOHOL – PAST AND PRESENT

Even if you're aiming to become a professional bartender, it's not absolutely essential to know a great deal about the history and varieties of alcohol. The majority of bar patrons are unlikely to confront you with questions like, "Hey, barkeep, how many different varietals does the Sonoma Valley produce?" or, "Say, what exactly is the chemical composition of this Heineken?" Nevertheless, it's a good idea to have at least a little gratuitous historical and technical knowledge on the subject. In this section, we try to address relevant subjects (although we often wax irrelevant), starting with the chemical process that creates alcohol and moving on to a short history of alcohol, followed by brief explanations of the various kinds of alcoholic beverages. The discussion of the alcohols will follow the order of the speed rail in hopes of reinforcing the more edifying sections of this chapter.

CHEMICALLY SPEAKING...

Liquor contains ethyl alcohol (ethanol), as opposed to methyl (wood) or isopropyl (rubbing) alcohol. Of the three varieties, only ethyl alcohol is safe to drink. Ethanol forms as the product of a chemical reaction known as fermentation, in which yeast enzymes decompose carbohydrates into carbon dioxide (CO_2) and ethanol (C_2H_5OH). These carbohydrates come from either grain (in the case of beer and most spirits) or fruit, especially grapes (in the case of wine and some spirits). The carbon dioxide can be left in the alcohol, as in beer, or allowed to evaporate into the atmosphere. In a strange twist of affairs, ethanol is also used to make fuel for running cars; at the same time, it is used by drinkers as a fuel to disenable their ability to drive.

A VERY, VERY BRIEF HISTORY OF ALCOHOL

Civilization begins with distillation.
William Faulkner

Faulkner was technically wrong – distillation didn't really come into vogue until the Middle Ages – but his point was correct; historically, almost all of the world's great civilizations have consumed alcohol in some form. Since

WILLIAM FAULKNER

It should probably be noted here that William Faulkner, while being the author of some of the most beautiful pieces of fiction in the American canon, has given his name to a phrase every average American slangster should have at the ready: The Faulkner Flu – or waking up in the morning with a groggy head and a sore throat from smoking cigarettes and drowning your muse in boxed wine.

13

its use pre-dates written history, no one knows who invented alcohol. In all likelihood, nor did the grunting inventor, although it is likely that he or she quickly came up with a word (or moaning iteration) to describe the hangover that quickly followed. There is some evidence that early agricultural societies enjoyed a very primitive form of alcohol by chewing and spitting out grain to let the mixture ferment; enzymes in the saliva converted the grain starch into sugar and eventually alcohol. While this proved satisfactory to nomads who knew not the meaning of bathing, you probably don't want to try it at home.

More palatable concoctions were developed by societies as far back as 10,000 years ago. At about that time, wine was first produced from grapes in Asia Minor. By 4000 B.C., societies had discovered viniculture. By 1000 B.C., the Egyptians, Phoenicians, and Chinese had caught on. The Greeks picked up the art of winemaking from the Egyptians and passed it on to the Romans, who during their imperial reign spread it amply throughout Europe and every pore of their body, leaving them vastly too drunk to continue to rule. Early beer production developed concurrently; in the Egypt of the pharaohs, beer-making was entrusted to the temple priests, inaugurating a longstanding association of alcohol with religion and mysticism (such as the Christian act of communion). Throughout the world, the type of alcohol produced depended upon the available resources. For example, African societies used millet to produce beer, the Japanese fermented rice into sake, and viniculture thrived in the Mediterranean and anywhere else that grapes could grow successfully. The English made mead out of honey, while in other parts of Europe barley was used to cultivate beer.

To the would-be martini drinkers of earlier millennia, fermentation had one drawback – the process did not yield beverages with an alcohol content higher than 12%. Distillation, the process of altering a substance through heating, was known to the Greeks and others but was not widely practiced. Then, about a thousand years ago, the Scots and Irish discovered that, by extracting much of the water from beer through distillation, they could produce a new, potent form of alcohol. They called it uisge beatha or usquebaugh, which evolved into today's word for whiskey. Throughout the British Isles, there was much rejoicing over this discovery, as toasts became more refined and hangovers became worse. ("Work," proclaimed Oscar Wilde, "is the curse of the drinking classes.") Soon alchemists all over Europe were experimenting with distillation and its products, affectionately known as aqua vitae, or "water of life" (not to be confused with Aquavit, a pernicious, herb-intensive, Swedish alcohol that is oft-described as liquid death). Early methods of distillation were rather crude, leaving a number of impurities in the liquor that they produced. It wasn't until the invention of the patent still in the early 19th century that it became possible to produce grain neutral spirits, from which most contemporary liquor is made.

Alcohol's position in modern life varies widely from country to country: the Bible,

for example, contains a large number of references to the production and consumption of wine. European societies almost unanimously embrace alcohol consumption as an act of hospitality and sociability; this is also true in Japan. Muslim societies, however frown upon the use of alcohol – its consumption is prohibited in the Koran, and in most Muslim nations it is illegal. Hindus take a less prohibitive but still negative attitude toward liquor.

In the United States, alcohol occupies a slightly ambivalent position. During Prohibition (1920-1933), the manufacture, sale, and distribution of alcohol were outlawed by the 18th Amendment to the Constitution. In political terms, Prohibition was a disaster – the use of alcohol by the public actually increased during this period, and poorly manufactured "moonshine" greatly increased the health risks associated with drinking. Prohibition is also widely blamed for the ascendancy of organized crime, as Beer Barons thrived on the vast black market created by the new laws. For drinkers, Prohibition brought with it a strangely exhilarating golden age of innovation, leading to the creation of a number of fine cocktails. Today, a variety of mostly Christian fundamentalist religious sects still proscribe the use of alcohol, and a number of "dry" counties in which it is illegal to sell alcohol still exist in some Southern states. That said, there is widespread acceptance of casual, controlled drinking, and scientific studies have now demonstrated that drinking in moderation – such as a daily glass of wine with dinner – can reduce the risk of various forms of heart disease. Aqua vitae indeed.

GIN

Deriving its name from the French genièvre, meaning "juniper berry," gin was originally prescribed as a diuretic. Although it has no officially sanctioned medicinal value today, some still swear that a couple of martinis can cure a wide variety of ailments. Of course, they generally die in a very prompt fashion. Gin is known as "a drinker's drink," meaning a lot of people can't stand the taste of it... and those who do like it generally find that all liquors make a fine drinker's drink.

Gin production involves several steps. First, grains (often corn and rye) are distilled into neutral spirits in a patent still. This grain alcohol is then flavored with juniper berries and other botanicals, distilled again, and bottled at 80 to 100 proof.

Gin brands may vary because of the quality of the raw ingredients, the purity of the added water, and the recipe of flavorings added prior to the second distillation. If you plan to add mixers, subtle brand variations won't matter much, so buy a cheaper brand. After you buy gin, keep the cap on the bottle or it may spoil. After seven to ten days without a cover, gin might taste milky; since it doesn't come from a mammal, that should provide some kind of instructive as to the need to throw away the bottle.

VODKA

Historians generally credit Poland and with the invention of vodka, perhaps as early as the 10th century. Russians, as has so often been their historical wont, plundered the recipe from Poland and gave it its name: zhizennia voda, meaning "water of life." After experiencing a great deal of existential angst at the lack of originality imparted to this title, the Russians eventually shortened the word to its affectionate diminutive, vodka, which translates literally as "dear little water."

Vodka production involves three basic steps. First, fermented carbohydrates (usually grain) are distilled to at least 190 proof (dear big water) in a patent still. The grain neutral spirits are then diluted, or "cut," with distilled water to a range of 80-100 proof, and then filtered through charcoal to remove all distinctive character, aroma, and taste.

This process makes it slightly more difficult to detect varia-

tions in quality among vodkas than other liquors. Nonetheless, brands of vodka still vary because of the quality of the raw materials, the purity of the water added, and the extent of the neutrality achieved by the charcoal filtration. As with gin, if you plan to combine the vodka with mixers, you can probably get away with using cheaper brands, as the mixer masks the slight imperfections of the less-crafted product… unless you're drinking an atrocious brand that turns its consumers into fire-breathing demons.

A relatively recent trend involves the flavoring of vodka. Vodka can be filtered through foreign juices to produce a distinct flavor, frequently a fruity one. This process is used in the creation of liquors such as Absolut Citron and other flavored vodkas. It should be mentioned that the flavoring process does not noticeably affect the alcohol content of vodka; although the liquor might taste different, it is still as potent as the real McCoy.

RUM

Rum production involves the same basic steps used in making many other liquors; sugarcane juice and molasses (the carbohydrates) are fermented, distilled, sometimes aged, often blended, and then bottled at 80 to 151 proof. Because of variations in this process, you could perhaps find as many kinds of rum as there are brands, but most differ primarily by country of origin.

Puerto Rican rums such as Bacardi, the most common in America, are light-bodied and dry. They are fermented with a special cultured yeast, then distilled in modern patent stills to over 160 proof (fairly neutral), aged at least one year, and blended with other aged rums. Some Puerto Rican rums have an amber or dark color due to aging in charred oak barrels rather than plain oak casks used for light rum. Virgin Island rums like Ron Virgin taste similar to Puerto Rican rum, but are slightly heavier and usually not aged.

Barbados rum such as Mount Gay also tastes heavier than Puerto Rican rum and has a darker color. Barbados rum is characterized by a soft, rather smoky flavor.

Jamaican rum such as Myers's is the darkest, richest variety. Whereas Puerto Rican production uses a cultured yeast, molasses for Jamaican rum is fermented naturally. Then it is distilled to less than 160 proof (which leaves some of the molasses flavor in the liquor), aged, often colored with caramel to darken the final product, and bottled at 80 to 100 proof.

Rum from other regions, such as Haiti (Rhum Barbancourt), Martinique, and New England (Caldwell's Newburyport) are much less common. All have their own unique characteristics.

Two other Puerto Rican rums merit special recognition. Some specialty drinks (Zombies, for example) call for 151-proof rum as an ingredient. Do not substitute 151-proof rum for regular bar rum (usually around 80 proof); it contains almost twice as much alcohol. On the other hand, spiced Puerto Rican rum, such as Captain Morgan's, can be used as a substitute for regular rum as requested by the drinker. It contains the same amount of alcohol, but with the addition of vanilla and other spices that impart more zest to the drink.

TEQUILA

Tequila is perhaps the most misunderstood of all liquors. Even some bar books still treat tequila as a mysterious Mexican potion full of worms, hallucinogens, and all manner of vile filth. In fact, tequila makers must adhere to strict government controls, which pretty much take all the mystery – and certainly the hallucinogens – out of the liquor. Tequila must be made from blue agave plants (Tequilana weber, blue variety) grown in a specific, government-designated area of Mexico (an area that includes the town of Tequila). It must go through two distilla-

WORMS AND TEQUILA

You'll find worms only in mescal (and sometimes basketball uniforms), not tequila. Mescal is another Mexican liquor, similar to tequila, but it is not subject to the same quality controls. Mescal may contain other varieties of the agave from any area of Mexico. The mescal worm is harmless and, despite the innuendos of mescal advertisers, contains no psychoactive elements... unless it's one of those crazy worms that spends its free time consuming peyote (perhaps that's how it ended up in the bottom of the bottle). Originally, distillers probably put it there because the worm spends its entire life cycle in the agave plant, so providing it with a ceremonial burial in mescal seemed like a polite thing to do. Today, the worm in the mescal bottle represents tradition or a shameless sales tactic depending upon your perspective.

tions and contain at least 51% fermented agave juice.

Production of tequila involves basically the same steps as other distilled spirits: a mixture of at least 51% blue agave juice and up to 49% sugarcane juice (the carbohydrates) is fermented, distilled twice in pot stills, filtered through charcoal, and then either bottled or aged for one to seven years. Aged tequila, called anejo, may be stored in used oak barrels, which provides its golden color. Tequila is 80 proof in the U.S., 96 proof in Mexico.

WHISKEYS

Whiskey, whisky, Scotch, Irish, Canadian, bourbon, rye, blended, straight – whiskeys come in wide and occasionally confusing varieties. Most differ by country of origin, primary base grain, or variations in processing. Some are more or less interchangeable – as a bartender, you should know enough about the different varieties so that you can substitute them in drinks when necessary.

Whiskey production involves four steps: malting, fermenting, distilling, and aging. That last step imparts color to the whiskey; colorless alcohol goes into wooden barrels to age, and interaction between the wood and the liquor supplies flavor, aroma, and color to the whiskey. As soon as whiskey is bottled, the aging stops.

Whiskey or whisky? Which spelling is correct? If you look at a bottle of Four Roses (American), for example, you will see the word whiskey. But if you glance at a bottle of Chivas Regal (Scottish), whisky is emblazoned on the label. As a rule, Scottish and Canadian distillers spell the word without the "e," and American and Irish whiskey producers include it.

The first qualitative difference is between straight and blended whiskeys. Some blended whiskeys contain mixtures of similar products made by different distillers at different times (as in Scotch); others have combinations of straight whiskeys and neutral, flavorless whiskeys (as in Canadian). Straight whiskeys, on the other hand, are not mixed at all, or are only mixed with whiskey from the same distillation period or distiller. The country of origin is a second important distinction. Scotch, Irish, Canadian, and American whiskeys are all made by different processes and, therefore, have very distinctive tastes.

Scotch, the whiskey of Scotland, usually has barley (and sometimes corn) as its primary base grain. Scotch tastes smoky, a flavor it acquires when the barley malt roasts over an open peat fire during the first step in production. Then this smoky-flavored malt is combined with water (the mash), fermented, distilled in a pot still, and aged at least three years in uncharred oak barrels or used sherry casks. All Scotches imported to the United States have aged at least four years; the best ones are 12 years old. Most contain blends of whiskies and have been bottled at 80 to 86 proof.

Irish whiskey, which includes whiskey made in Northern Ireland, uses barley and other grains as its primary bases. Its ingredients and the methods used to make it are similar to those of Scotch. During Irish whiskey production, however, the malt roasts over coal-fired kilns, so Irish whiskey does not have Scotch's smoky flavor. Sometimes the Irish blend their whiskies for a lighter product. It is then aged five to ten years in used sherry casks and bottled at 86 proof.

American whiskeys include bourbon, rye, corn, bottled-in-bond, sour mash, and blended. Bourbon, named for Bourbon County, Kentucky, where this whiskey originates, is distilled from a fermented mash of at least 51% rye grain in its mash. The balance of the mash may contain any other grain, usually rye and barley. The aging process takes two to 12 years in oak barrels, after which the bourbon is bottled at 80 to 90 proof. Rye whiskey contains at least 51% rye grain in its mash. Real rye whiskey (such as Old Overholt) is not as popular as it once was, though, so it usually stays on the back bar. Be alert to this when worldly sophisticates order "rye and ginger," for example; they probably want blended whiskey (such as Seagram's 7 or VO). Odd as it may seem, a person who wants to drink real rye usually has to say so rather emphatically: "I want rye – I mean real rye, not that yuppie dishwater you're serving the kids." Corn whiskey is distilled from a fermented mash of grain containing at least 80% corn. Notice the difference between bourbon (51% corn) and corn whiskey (80%). In the U.S., bottled-in-bond whiskey is straight whiskey that was bottled at 100 proof and aged at least four years in U.S. government-bonded warehouses. Sour mashes contain some proportion of previously fermented yeast (as opposed to mash, which is made only from fresh yeast). Jack Daniel's Tennessee Whiskey is made from a sour mash.

The difference between straight and blended American whiskeys may seem confounding. Straight means that the mash must contain at least 51% of a certain grain:

MASH	WHISKEY
51% barley	straight malt whiskey
51% rye	straight rye whiskey
51% corn	straight bourbon whiskey
80% corn	straight corn whiskey

Blended whiskeys are made from combinations of similar straight whiskeys from different distillations or distillers.

The choice of "the right whiskey" (or whisky) depends on your preference. At a party, most hosts will provide at least two: Scotch and bourbon (and usually also a blended selection). Professional bars stock a variety of whiskeys (including at least three on the speed rail), so there you'll have a better chance of finding your favorite type and brand. Every brand of whisky varies in flavor according to its base grains, production techniques, and aging, so it is impossible to generalize about which is best. More expensive brands have probably been made with high-quality grains, careful production regulations (for a consistently good whiskey), and longer aging periods. On the other hand, some expensive brands owe their premium price tags in part to having been heavily advertised so that people will pay for their image. Bars, of course, also charge more for these prestige brands.

BRANDY

> *Claret is the liquor for boys; port for men; but he who aspires to be a hero must drink brandy.*
> Samuel Johnson

While it is generally relegated to the world of after-dinner drinks (and hence absent on the speed rail), brandy is still a popular – or at least infamous – drink of aspiring sophisticates. In particular, it is associated with the ancient tradition of men adjourning for an after-dinner cigar and brandy. It is distilled from wine or a fermented fruit mash. If it is made from wine (that is, from grapes), the name brandy stands alone, but if it is distilled from another fruit, brandy is called by the fruit name. For example, apricot brandy contains an apricot base. Some brandies, however, have special names. Cognac, usually considered the finest of brandies, comes from the Cognac region of France. Armagnac, another fine brandy, comes from the Gers region of France. Metaxa is a sweet, dark, grape-based, Greek brandy. Ouzo, another Greek product, is colorless and tastes like licorice. Calvados, an apple brandy from the Calvados region of France, is similar to applejack and American apple brandy. Kirschwasser, or kirsch, is a clear, cherry brandy of European origin. Grappa is a dry, colorless, grape-based, Italian brandy.

LIQUEURS

Liqueurs (or cordials) were originally invented as aphrodisiacs; alas, like the worms in a bottle of tequila, this is a lot of nonsense. Today's liqueurs contain various plants, fruits, and other flavorings, and are often very colorful. All contain at least 2.5% sugar, but most have much more than that. In fact, the prefix crème de, as in crème de menthe and crème de cacao, refers to the high sugar content of the liqueurs, which gives them a creamy consistency.

Liqueurs of the same flavor base generally congregate on the back bar. To help you learn which ones taste similar, and can therefore be interchanged when necessary, the following list offers a partial grouping of common liqueurs according to flavor.

While our list is admittedly incomplete, we've tried to include all of the variants of alcohol that you will encounter in the rest of the guide. New liqueurs and drinks, however, do not follow the guidelines that we've established, and a good bartender must stay atop current trends and new products. However, don't forget your most valuable gauge of new trends – the customer. If you keep your ears to the ground in a bar and try to learn the newfangled recipes of the hipsters, everything should be peachy-keen.

HIPSTERS

While your average run-of-the-mill hipster might ask for some kind of liqueur, the chic and the happening will more than likely get a gin and tonic or a manhattan.

NUTTY FLAVORS

Amaretto – almond
Crème de noyaux – almond
Crème de almond – for obvious reasons, almond
Frangelico – hazelnut

Amaretto di Saronno is a high-quality, rather expensive, amber-colored liqueur, delicious on its own, in mixed drinks, and in coffee. You may substitute other brands to save money in some drinks, but choose carefully, as many do not taste the same as the original. Crème d'almond and crème de noyaux are similar; you can interchange these red liqueurs in mixed drinks if necessary.

Frangelico is a more infrequently used liqueur, and can't really be substituted for the other varieties, although it's every bit as tasty as these almondy flavors.

COFFEE

Kahlúa
Tia Maria
Coffee brandy

You can sometimes interchange these and other similar products in mixed drinks, either to save money or when you've run out of something. People often order Kahlúa by name, but if they don't (in a drink such as a White Russian or Sombrero), use coffee brandy. Tia Maria contains Jamaican rum with coffee flavoring, and also provides a reasonable substitute for Kahlúa in a pinch.

BERRIES

Black Haus – blackberry
Boggs – cranberry
Chambord – black raspberry
Cranberria – cranberry
Crème de cassis – black currant
Maraschino – cherry
Sloe gin – sloe berry

Sloe gin, neither sloe nor gin, obtains its flavor from sloe berries, the fruit of the blackthorn bush. This red liqueur is popular in Sloe Gin Fizzes and Sloe Screws.

While very few people have ever heard of or cared about Black Haus, it is one of the tastiest varieties of schnapps that the hallowed halls of the Harvard Bartending School have ever dared to contain. And they have a very bizarre website (http://www.blackhaus.com)

FRUITS OF THE VINE

Cocoribe – coconut
Cointreau – orange
Crème de banane – banana
Curaçao – orange
Grand Marnier – orange
Malibu – coconut
Midori – melon
Peach schnapps – peach
Pisang Ambon – bitter orange
Triple sec – orange

This clear and bittersweet Cointreau and the orange-colored, co-gnac-based Grand Marnier are both name-brand orange liqueurs. Curaçao comes in both orange and a pretty blue. Make sure that you use orange when no color is specified and blue when the recipe demands its use. Triple sec, a clear, tart liqueur, is not as sweet as Curaçao. When a recipe calls for Cointreau, you can substitute triple sec if it proves to be more convenient or less expensive. Pisang Ambon is a green, bitter, orange-and-spice flavored, Dutch liqueur.

Many other melon liqueurs have appeared on the market in the wake of Midori's success. Taste them before trying to substitute, just to make sure that they're up to snuff; many aren't as good, but some will blend nicely in mixed drinks.

HERBS, SPICES, AND OTHER SUCH VICES

Aquavit – caraway
Benedictine – mystery
Campari – bittersweet
Jägermeister – herbs and spices
Kümmel – caraway
Chartreuse – saffron or chlorophyll
Crème de menthe – mint
Crème de violette – violet
Crème Yvette – violet
Drambuie – honey

Parfait Amour – violet
Pimm's No. 1 – herbs, spices, and fruits
Peppermint schnapps – mint

Benedictine and Chartreuse both date from the 16th century and contain exotic blends of many herbs and spices. Green Chartreuse is flavored with chlorophyll, while yellow Chartreuse contains a lighter and sweeter saffron flavor. Benedictine, produced by monks who will defend the honor and secrecy of their beverage by killing anyone who pirates it, use a cognac base flavored with any number of mysterious herbs, spices, and fruit peels. Campari is a bittersweet, amber, Italian liqueur. Pimm's No. 1 contains herbs, spices, and various fruits in its blend. Jägermeister (literally: hunting master) contain a fully loaded blend of 56 herbs and spices, although it is surprisingly sweet.

Aquavit and Kümmel are unique in that they are strong drinks that disgust many without even being elevated to the exclusive pantheon of "drinker's drinks." Kümmel is flavored with caraway, cumin, and fennel while Aquavit is made from potatoes and then flavored with caraway seeds.

Crème de menthe comes in two colors, green and white (clear). Many people drink it as an after-dinner cordial, or between courses of a meal as a palate cleanser. Consider color in deciding which crème de menthe to put in a drink. Fortuitously, many recipes specify a color.

The violet liqueurs (crème de violette, Crème Yvette, and Parfait Amour) are violet-flavored and -colored.

Drambuie is a honey- and herb-sweetened variety of Scotch.

LICORICE AND ANISE
Absinthe
Anisette
Galliano
Ouzo
Pernod
Sambuca

There have been many debates about licorice vs. anise. In general, Anise is a sweet tasting, aromatic herb. Licorice has a similar, but considerably stronger, aroma along with a sweet but more medicinal taste.

Absinthe contains a dangerous narcotic ingredient (wormwood) as well as a Herculean quantity of liquor (136 proof) and is illegal in the United States, although any number of blind madder-than-hell French writers attest to the fact that it is not prohibited everywhere. Law-abiding residents of the U.S. use Pernod as a substitute. Some advice from someone who has sampled the bitter joy of absinthe: there are different ways to take your absinthe. Some strain it through sugar into a glass and then sip it up slowly. Others, and perhaps the more adventurous, know that absinthe is not only a mind-altering narcotic, but also an alcohol of very high proof. Thus, daredevils will put a shot of absinthe into a shot glass and light it on fire, finally sucking the vile liquid through specially-designed extra long straws. Absinthe supposedly will allow you to "see the world as you want it" after a shot, and "see the world as it really is" after two shots. However, after seven shots, you will feel like vomiting, and see the world like a retching sucker. Be warned.

Galliano, a golden, vanilla-licorice liqueur, comes in a very tall bottle and goes into drinks containing the word Golden, such as a Golden Dream or a Golden Cadillac.

CREAM
Bailey's Irish Cream
Belle Bonne
McGuire's Original Cream
Myers's Rum Cream
Toasted almond cream
Venetian Cream

Sweet cream liqueurs contain cream, alcohol, and flavorings. The alcohol preserves the cream so that the liqueur can be stored and served at any temperature. In a sense, these liqueurs are pre-mixed cream cocktails, so they usually contain relatively little alcohol.

CHAPTER 2:
TOYS & TRINKETS

If you've never worked at a fully stocked bar before, your first encounter with this vast world might be somewhat bewildering. No one led you to expect a brave, new, technological world that makes the special effects in *Star Wars* seem basic by comparison. Surely George Lucas would not dare to be so bold as to produce the dizzying array of glasses or a bizarre appliance that looks like the result of an unholy matrimony of a Slinky and a spatula, unless he was seeking a new superweapon meant to annihilate the Ewoks.

Relax. None of these strange objects can hurt you, nor are they as complicated as they might seem at first glance. A few simple guidelines will allow you to master the different glasses in no time at all. And that funny looking thing? It's a cocktail strainer. Perfectly harmless (unless you sympathize with the ice struggling to find its way into a drink; the ice deserves no sympathy).

In this chapter, we'll explain the various contraptions that keep things running smoothly at any bar, offering brief descriptions of the various utensils, glassware, and garnishes that you'll need to tend bar.

UTENSILS

Bartenders usually keep a variety of tools around to help them do everything from shaking to straining to pouring. The most basic and useful utensils comprise what we like to call the "bartending kit"; most bartenders would never try to work without them. (Blatant self-promotion – Order your own official Harvard Student Agencies Bartending Kit to be just like one of the pros! For more information, see the ad the end of this book.)

A basic kit contains:

SHAKER SET: Bartenders use a shaker to make whiskey sours, daiquiris, margaritas, and the other popular shaken drinks listed in

Chapter 3. We prefer a steel shell for the outer part and a glass shaker that fits inside. Glass works best for the inner part because some recipes ask you to "eye-ball" the right amount of liquor in a drink, and glass allows you to see how much you pour. Shakers come in many shapes and sizes; our Bartending Kit uses a 12 oz. shaker because it allows the bartender to prepare several servings of a drink at once. However, use what is comfortable for you and allows you to make drinks with the greatest speed and efficiency.

STRAINERS: The  strainer fits over the shaker so that you can pour the chilled drink into a glass without the ice cubes. This type of drink is referred to as "straight up," as in a martini straight up.

SPEEDPOURERS: Speedpourers fit into the mouth of a bottle and dispense the liquor at an even rate. As you will see in Chapter 3, these gadgets are essential for the speed-oriented bartender. Make sure to put the speedpourer in the bottle at a right angle to the label; with all the pourers facing the same way, you can quickly grab each bottle without having to check the direction of the stream of liquor. If you position the bottles this way, customers are able to read the label as you pour, and it also ensures that the liquor flows at an even rate.

BAR SPOON: The recommended bar spoon looks like the one shown here, with a long, twirled handle and a small spoon at the end. This type of spoon serves three purposes: you can stir drinks with the handle, pour alcohol carefully down the twirled segment or onto the back of the spoon (when making layered shots, for example), and pick up fruit with the spoon. Although busy bartenders rarely follow the rule, the law in some states prohibits the handling of fruit garnishes, so the spoon is made for those bartenders who haven't gotten so big in their breeches that they think of themselves as "above the law."

COMBINATION CORKSCREW/ BOTTLE OPENER / CAN OPENER: This tool proves to be highly efficient because three separate pieces can get lost too easily at a hectic bar. You should choose whatever feels most comfortable. If you have a pocketknife with 1800 gadgets, you can also amuse yourself amply if your shift turns dull.

JIGGER/PONY: The larger end is the jigger, which measures 1½ oz.; the smaller end is the pony, which measures 1 oz. Although sometimes quite handy, a jigger/pony or other measuring glass will become unnecessary after you're accustomed to using speedpourers. Some bars, however, insist that employees use measuring glasses to

ensure that they don't pour too much and waste liquor. Additionally, greenhorn bartenders are advised to use the jigger and pony for a good little while to standardize their three-count (the three-count is discussed at greater length in "Measuring").

The following items are also useful:

ICE BUCKET: Bucket, basin, bag, or whatever you have around for holding ice – anything clean is fine.

ICE SCOOP or **TONGS:** They are nice for some occasions, though impractical in a busy bar.

KNIFE: You will need a knife to cut up fruit garnishes.

SCOOPING ICE

Never Never NEVER Ever scoop up ice with a glass; instead, always use either an ice scoop, tongs, or your hand. Scooping ice with a glass is a big safety hazard, especially since broken glass will seamlessly disappear into its icy counterpart. So dangerous is this frosty threat that state law often mandates the use of an ice scoop or tongs.

GLASSWARE

The following list (complete with illustrations) will familiarize you with some glassware options available at bars. For the home, purchase any or all of them. In a professional establishment, the manager usually decides which glass to use for each drink. These illustrations are merely examples of different types; you'll find many variations and creative adaptations from bar to bar. Be careful, however, and don't get too creative. Remember that the right glass makes quite a difference in the final appearance of a drink – wine loses some of its appeal in a beer mug (unless you're serving the wine out of a box), and a piña colada won't fit in a shot glass (assuming that your servings aren't ridiculously stingy).

33

HIGHBALL: Used for more drinks than any other glass (for all those gin and tonics, Scotch and waters, etc.), highballs vary considerably from bar to bar. Most are clear, tall glasses that hold between 8 and 12 oz.

LOWBALL: Also used for many drinks, lowball or "on-the-rocks" glasses come to 9 oz. and are best for drinks served on the rocks, such as a martini on the rocks, Scotch on the rocks, a Black Russian, and many others.

OLD FASHIONED: This 4 to 7 oz. glass looks similar to an on-the-rocks glass, but has a bump in the base to remind the bartender to prepare the sugar, water, and bitters mixtures for an Old Fashioned. Today, many bars use these to double duty as on-the-rocks glasses.

COLLINS: Best for Collinses, sloe gin fizzes, and Singapore Slings, these 12 oz. glasses are frosted with some clear glass left at the top to remind the bartender to add soda water to the top of a Collins. They lend a cool, refreshing image to these drinks.

COCKTAIL/WHISKEY SOUR: Martinis, Manhattans, and other cocktails ordered straight up are initially prepared with ice and then strained into a 4 oz. cocktail glass. Sours are prepared in the same way and strained into a 4 oz. sour glass. The stem on these glasses enables the drinker to hold the glass without warming the chilled contents.

WINE: Wine glasses come in a wide array of shapes and sizes. Choose yours according to your own preferences.

CHAMPAGNE: Champagne glasses come in two shapes and sizes. The American glass, by far the most popular here, is very wide and shallow and holds 4 to 6 oz. The European glass, tall and fluted, has a 7 to 11 oz. capacity for more hearty imbibing. The European glass is better for champagne than its American counterpart, and not just because it holds more volume. The tapered mouth of the European glass has less surface area, and thus holds the bubbles in longer (unlike the American glass, which allows the bubbles to dissipate quickly). Also, the European glass causes less spillage. Of course, what's a New Year's Eve without a few drinks spilled on you?

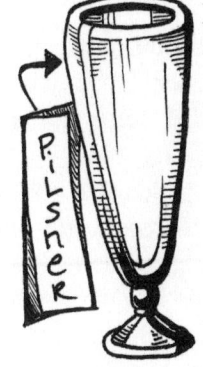

BEER: Usually holding about 10 oz., beer glasses come in two basic shapes – the mug and the Pilsner glass. Most people have already seen mugs. The Pilsner-style glass was invented for use with Pilsner beer, but it is actually suitable for any kind of beer. Bar managers often prefer mugs because they do not break as easily as the Pilsners.

SHOT: These 1 to 3 oz. glasses can be used to serve shots of liquor or to measure alcohol.

LIQUEUR: Also known as a "pony," this 1 oz. glass is appropriate for after-dinner liqueurs and layered shots.

SHERRY: Serve sherry, port, or aperitifs like Dubonnet in 2½ to 3½ oz. glasses.

BRANDY: Brandy snifters range in capacity from 5 to 25 oz. All have basically the same shape, and are designed to be cupped by the hand to warm the brandy.

The technology of containers can be as variegated as the drinks that fill them – coconut shells in Polynesian restaurants, free tumblers from the gas station, glasses with big mouse ears from that vacation in Orlando…. The innovations never stop. In the absence of any receptacle, one can always drop a bottle into a paper bag and start swigging. Of course, such actions are not the ones that you will generally want to encourage as a bartender.

GARNISHES & GARBAGE

Just as the right glassware can make a cocktail look infinitely more appealing, those additions the bartender puts in a drink can also make it look – and taste – better.

The words "garnish" and "garbage" refer to the fruits and vegetables that you drop in a drink. Although many bartenders use the two words interchangeably, they have different technical meanings. Garnishes change the taste of a drink, such as a lime wedge in a gin and tonic or a lemon twist in a bourbon. Garbage just makes the drink look pretty, such as a cherry in a Manhattan or an orange slice and pineapple chunk in a piña colada. Here are some garnishes and garbage commonly found on a bar.

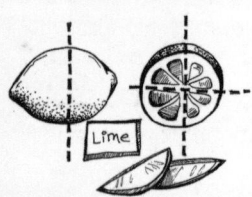

LIME WEDGES: Cut the lime in half (through its equator) and then quarter each half, following the natural contours of the fruit, to make eight wedges. Squeeze the lime over the drink, rub it around the edges of the glass if you so desire, and drop it in. Lime wedges are popular garnishes in many drinks, so keep plenty on hand. If you start to run low on limes, cut smaller wedges, but make sure you don't run out.

LIME WHEELS: Starting at the stem, cut the lime in half. Lay each half with the flat side down, and cut width-wise to make semicircular, fan-like slices. Make a little cut down the middle of each slice so that you can slide it onto the rim of the glass.

LEMON TWISTS: Cut off the two ends of the lemon. Make a lengthwise incision into the lemon's peel (between the two ends that you just cut off), then, with a spoon, separate the fruit from its peel. (You just use the peel in the drink.) Slice the peel lengthwise into ¼ in. wide strips. Twist the peel over

the drink, rub it around the edge of the glass, drop it in, and stir. It's a good idea to keep some lemon slices or wedges at the bar, in case some fussy drinkers drop by who prefer a more lemony taste. Generally, you won't need to use too many lemon twists over the course of a night; cutting up one lemon peel at the beginning of the evening should do the trick.

ORANGE SLICES: Starting at the stem, cut the orange in half. Lay each half with the flatside down, and cut widthwise to make semicircular, fan-like slices. Make a little cut down the middle of each slice so that you can slide it onto the rim of the glass.

CHERRIES: Use stemmed maraschino cherries in your cocktails. Drinkers like stems, since they allow the cherry to be easily snapped out of the glass… and because they like to do tricks tying cherry stems in their mouths.

OLIVES: A must for martini drinkers, olives should be green, pitted, and without pimento.

ONIONS: Get little cocktail onions for your Gibson – unless you don't know anyone who drinks Gibsons. Not many people do.

The wide variety of condiments and other flavorings in a well-stocked bar include:

SUGAR: Buy superfine, granulated sugar, which mixes more easily in drinks and won't leave a syrupy layer on the bottom of the glass.

SIMPLE SYRUP: An alternative to dry sugar. Some bartenders prefer to make simple syrup by mixing sugar and water together. Heat one pound of sugar in one quart of water until it dissolves. Keep it in a bottle with a speedpourer in it.

SALT: Keep a plate of rock, not table, salt on hand for making Salty Dogs and Margaritas.

GRENADINE: This red, non-alcoholic, sugar-and-pomegranate syrup colors and sweetens drinks.

BITTERS: As the name suggests, this mixer is bitter and infrequently used in drinks these days except in Old Fashioneds. You can add it to Manhattans or Bloody Mary's if you like. Note that bitters is alcoholic and should not be used in non-alcoholic drinks, and even a few drops can be harmful to some non-drinkers.

BLOODY MARY CONDIMENTS: Keep any or all of the following on hand for bloodies: Tabasco sauce, Worcestershire sauce, salt and pepper, horseradish, celery stalks. Some bars or servers like to keep pre-fabbed Bloddy Mary mix on hand to avoid the time-consuming hassle of preparing it when ordered.

NUTMEG: For Brandy Alexanders and eggnogs.

And, of course, most importantly:
ICE… and lots of it.

This rather extensive list of garnishes and condiments should give you an idea of the kinds of ingredients to expect in Chapter 3. Don't run out to the store and buy every one of them, however; just pick and choose according to your preferences.

CHAPTER 3:
MASTERING MIXOLOGY

Most Bartending guides fall all over themselves trying to convince you that their book contains more drink recipes than the competition's. "Contains All the Drink Recipes Ever Invented!"... "Over 400,000 Recipes!" they proudly exclaim. Such claims hold only trivial merits, since you'll only really encounter about 50 or 100 of those thousands of wacky, wild recipes on a regular basis. More important is to learn the processes by which all of the drinks can be made, since you can always just ask a customer how, exactly, one concocts a "Tropical Wild Fuzzy Passionate Screw." Most drinks are so outlandish that customers will quickly retreat, changing their request to something a bit more manageable, such as a gin and tonic, while those who maintain a strong attachment to their obscure beverage will likely know the ingredients, having triumphed in their little game of "stump the bartender." Don't worry about memorizing these recipes unless your regular customers are ordering drinks with which you aren't familiar.

As luck would have it, most aspiring mixologists already have a pretty good grasp of the most important drinks that they'll need to learn how to make. Gin and tonic, Scotch and soda, rum and Coke, screwdriver... sound familiar? These drinks are basic highballs, which comprise at least 70% of all drinks a typical bartender serves. While some highballs might require a little extra effort, most are incredibly simple once you know the basic technique.

MEASURING

The following techniques provide relatively successful means of measuring alcohol into a drink:

METHOD 1: THE THREE COUNT: Fast as Carl Lewis and smooth as velour, the three-count technique provides the least cumbersome means of confronting alcohol measurement. The speedpourers that you stuff into a bottle's mouth allow alcohol to flow out at an even rate. If you grab the bottle by the neck, turn it completely upside down over the glass, and count to three at the right speed, you can measure out exactly 1½ oz. Get a bottle of colored water, put a speedpourer in it, and keep practicing until you get a cadence that measures exactly 1½ oz., or ½ oz. per count, into a jigger. Remember to grab the bottle firmly by the neck (place your index finger against speedpourer for extra leverage, but be sure not to cover the air hole) for extra control. Practice repeatedly until you get it right. After a while, you won't even have to count anymore, as a three count will eventually feel right to you. Once you develop a good count, you can use the cadence for all the other necessary quantities.

METHOD 2: THE TWO-FINGER TECHNIQUE: Put your two fingers together around the bottom of the highball glass and then pour in until it reaches the top of your fingers. This method is faster than the jigger glass routine, but inaccurate; bartenders with bony fingers serve weak drinks while fat-fingered types will quickly becomes a drinker's best friend!

METHOD 3: RIDE THE JIGGER, NOT THE PONY: Measure the liquor in a jigger and then pour it into the drink. This method is accurate, but too slow and cumbersome if you're working at a crowded bar. Some bar managers insist that their employees use this method to ensure that no liquor is wasted. If you must follow this procedure, here's a way to pour faster and make customers think they're getting a stronger drink. First, hold the jigger glass in one hand and the liquor bottle in the other. Pour less than 1½ oz. into the jigger glass, and then dump that into the highball glass while also pouring a little more liquor from the bottle. To the customer, it appears as though you gave them a full jigger plus another splash from the bottle in each drink. They will be pleased and probably tip you more. This is also a clever bit of deception to employ if a customer is complaining that her drinks are too weak.

HOW TO USE THE RECIPE GUIDE

Most of these recipes are categorized according to how they're made. This setup enables you to learn and remember the method at the same time that you see the actual recipe. If you want to make a specific drink, you can find it in the index. Below we have listed 12 main categories of drinks, divided into separate chapters according to the frequency with which you'll be asked to make these concoctions. The first three categories contain three subgroups: Basics, Populars, and Funs. Basic drinks are the old standbys, such as a gin and tonic in the highball section, martinis in the stirred, and daiquiris in the shaken section. Popular drinks aren't quite as classic but do require memorization if you plan to work in a bar someday. Fun drinks include many you've never heard of before and may never need again, so you don't need to memorize them. Fun drinks are arranged alphabetically. The categories are:

Chapter 3: Mastering Mixology
1. Highballs
     Basic (memorize)
     Popular (memorize if you plan to work in a bar)
     Fun Drinks (no need to memorize, arranged alphabetically)
2. Stirred Cocktails
     Basic
     Popular
     Fun Drinks
3 Shaken Cocktails
     Basic
     Popular
     Fun Drinks
4. Blended Drinks
5. Shots
     Mixed Shots
     Layered Shots

HIGHBALLS

Highballs are defined technically as an iced drink containing liquor and water or a carbonated beverage and served in a tall glass. In the case of tending bar, however, the usage defines a different, broader meaning, in which highballs are considered to be those drinks served on ice with any old kind of mixers that you can prepare directly in a 9 oz. highball glass (unless, of course, you prefer another, more creative presentation). Basic highballs are the most common ones you will serve, whether in a bar or at home. Fortuitously, they are also the easiest to make. Memorize them. It's easy – they are arranged by type of liquor used to help you remember the ingredients.

To make highballs, follow these easy steps (on the following page):

HIGHBALLS

Drinks with the word "highball" in their name, according to common usage, contain ginger ale as a main ingredient. By this time, you know better – highballs are supposed to refer to a much broader classification of drinks (namely, all of the drinks in this section). Nevertheless, do not revel in your potential consumer's ignorance. Such an act is considered "impolite" and might mean that you'll have either your tip or the so called "highball" thrown in your face.

1. Fill a highball glass two-thirds full with ice. Always do this using an ice scooper or your hands, never with the glass.
2. Pour in one jigger (1½ oz.) of liquor. Some bars prefer to save money by serving only 1 oz. highballs, however.
3. Pour mixer to the top. If you pour too little, it looks like you're skimping. If you are skimping, find a way to do so discreetly. If you are caught, however, never lie about it while under oath to a grand jury – bartender's reputations can be impeached, too.
4. If the mixer is non-carbonated, stir it, or stick a straw in it and let the drinker stir it. With carbonated mixers, do not stir. The bubbles do the mixing, and stirring tends to make the carbonation go flat.
5. Garnish the drink, if necessary.

A bartending shortcut exists for producing several drinks at a time. It's fairly easy to do, but wholly unnecessary to learn unless you plan on working in a bar someday. If you want to make three gin and tonics, for example, follow these directions:

1. Line up three ice-filled glasses in a row with their rims touching.
2. Turn the gin bottle over the first glass for a three-count, then just move the bottle quickly over to the second glass and then the third.
3. Pour tonic in the three glasses.
4. Squeeze limes into the drinks.

The next time you go to a bar, watch the bartender and you'll learn professional hints. Don't worry too much about exactitude – while you can't substitute whiskey for water or vodka for vermouth (unless you don't mind a quick slap in the face from an angry patron), the world will keep on turnin' even if you accidentally pour an extra half ounce of liquor into a drink. As evidence of this, notice how often recipes for the same drink differ from one bar book to another, or from one bar to the next. Hey man, this is bartending, and all truths are relative.

BASIC HIGHBALLS

Gin and Tonic
1½ oz. gin
tonic to fill
garnish with a lime wedge

Gin Highball
1½ oz. gin
ginger ale to fill
garnish with a lemon twist

Gin Buck
1½ oz. gin
juice of ½ lemon
ginger ale to fill

Gin Rickey
1½ oz. gin
soda water to fill
garnish with a lemon twist

This is the only gin and clear mixer garnished with a lemon twist – most call for a lime wedge.

Gin and Orange Juice
1½ oz. gin
orange juice to fill

This drink is fairly self-explanatory, although some folks try to make it a more nuanced experience by referring to it as a "left-handed screwdriver."

SODA WATER

Soda and tonic water are not easily confused with wine. Just in case you need a refresher, these two mixers are generally carbonated, wine generally is not. Many beginning bartenders seem hell-bent on minimizing this fundamental distinction, however, as they let their giant bottles of soda water and tonic water breathe. But vicious irony of ironies, tonic and soda water, when left to breathe, quickly die, going flat with exceptional speed once opened. Do not be victimized by the short lifespan of carbonation! Always re-cap your, bottles, put them in the refrigerator when you're not using them, and buy smaller bottles if you're not serving large numbers of people.

Greyhound
1½ oz. gin
grapefruit juice to fill

Again, beware the intricacies of the drinker's vocabulary. To avoid confusion, many people will simply ask for a gin and grapefruit juice when they desire this specific recipe. Blessed are they. However, when invoking the term "greyhound," many drinkers want vodka as the main ingredient when hoping to experience this fast, smooth puppy.

SALTING THE EDGES

Rimming your glass with salt is a lot easier than trying to garnish a small yet ferocious animal. The following three easy steps should provide for a successfully salted drinking vessel:
1. Pour rock salt on a plate. Kosher salt generally works best, as its crystals are bigger and cling to the glass with much greater ease.
2. Rub a lime wedge around the rim of the glass.
3. Roll the rim of the glass in salt

Salty Dog
Salt the glass
1½ oz. gin
grapefruit juice to fill

Pour this drink into a highball glass rimmed with salt. Vodka is sometimes substituted for gin in this drink – always ask a drinker which breed of dog they prefer. This one is easy to remember, as it's merely a greyhound with a salted glass.

VODKA

Vodka and Tonic
1½ oz. vodka
tonic water to fill
garnish with a lime wedge

Vodka Highball

1½ oz. vodka
ginger ale to fill
garnish with a lime wedge

Screwdriver

1½ oz. vodka
orange juice to fill

Madras

1½ oz. vodka
orange juice to ¼ fill
cranberry juice to fill

Dribble cranberry juice around the top to give a blotchy appearance. Don't stir. This drink might remind you of a bright madras plaid.

Cape Codder

1½ oz. vodka
cranberry juice to fill
garnish with a lime wedge

Seabreeze

1½ oz. vodka
grapefruit juice to ¾ fill
cranberry juice to fill

Stir. This drink is a pretty pink color.

Vodka "7"

1½ oz. vodka
7-Up, Sprite, or any lemon-lime soda to fill
garnish with a cherry and an orange slice

MNEMONICS

Many aspiring bartenders are afflicted with heart palpitations when confronted with the seemingly limitless domain of alcoholic delights. Fortunately for those of you who have devoted a lifetime to memorizing the statistics of the '61 Yankees, we've come up with any number of mnemonic devices geared toward helping you preserve cherished cranial capacity for generally irrelevant information. If you can't remember that cranberries grow on Cape Cod, Massachusetts, try to learn alliterative linkages – Cape Codder and cranberry juice sure do have a bunch of C's!

THE BLOODY MARY

"Bloody" drinkers have diverse tastes, so you should ask if the drinker would like the drink hot, and alter accordingly with Tabasco sauce. There are about as many different recipes for Bloody Marys as there are drinkers. Some prefer gin to vodka, and any number of interesting ingredients may be added or substituted to make that perfect, customized Bloody Mary. You can experiment with clam juice, dill, basil, garlic, curry powder, or barbecue sauce (yee-haw!). Feel free to be creative; you may be the bartender who discovers the perfect combination!

Bloody Mary

1½ oz. vodka
tomato juice to ¾ fill
small splash lemon juice
dash Worcestershire sauce
dash Tabasco sauce (more for a hotter drink)
shake of salt and pepper
¼ tsp. horseradish (optional)
garnish with a lime or (for the more ambitious
    and vegetably inclined) a celery stick

Shake all of these ingredients with ice, then strain into a glass filled with ice.

RUM

Rum and Tonic

1½ oz. rum
tonic water to fill
garnish with a lime wedge

Rum and Coke

1½ oz. rum
cola (or diet cola) to fill

Cuba Libre

1½ oz. rum
cola to fill
garnish with a lime wedge

Cuba Libre ("Free Cuba") is just a fancy name for a rum and cola with a lime wedge, although to true revolutionaries, it has a much stronger meaning and is often accompanied by the singing of one anthem or another. Nuts to Castro!

Rum Highball

1½ oz. rum

ginger ale to fill

garnish with a lemon twist

Soda water can be substituted for ginger ale in this variation on a "highball."

Rum and Orange Juice

1½ oz. light rum

orange juice to fill

This drink is sometimes called a rum screwdriver.

Rum and Pineapple Juice

1½ oz. rum

pineapple juice to fill

Rum Cooler

1½ oz. rum

7-Up, Sprite, or soda water to fill

garnish with a lemon wedge

WHISKEY

The following highballs can contain bourbon, blended whiskey, Scotch, or some other whiskey. The drinker will tell the bartender what to put in – Scotch and water, for instance. Often with these dark alcohols, drinkers prefer to choose a brand, such as Dewar's and soda instead of just Scotch and soda.

Dealing with the many different kinds of whiskey often frustrates and confuses new bartenders, or even a drinker of light alcohols for that matter. If you fit into either of these categories, read over the whiskey section of Chapter 1 before trying to serve these drinks.

WHISKEY

Some whiskey drinkers belong to the very devout kingdom of straight Scotch. Do not cross these people; follow their instructions rigorously. They'll often order a Scotch on the rocks or blended whiskey with just a splash of, water. Some will request a brand, such as "J&B neat" (remember that "neat" means straight out of the bottle with no ice). Serve these drinks in rock glasses. The garnish for dark alcohols is usually a lemon twist, both for lowballs (rocks) and highballs. With sweet mixers, leave out the twist!

Whiskey and Water
1½ oz. whiskey
water to fill
garnish with a lemon twist.

Some people request only a splash of water. A splash equals ½ oz., so just put a little water in (no need to measure) and serve it in a rocks glass.

Whiskey and Soda
1½ oz. whiskey
soda water to fill
garnish with a lemon twist

Whiskey Highball
1½ oz. whiskey
ginger ale to fill

Presbyterian
1½ oz. whiskey (usually blended)
equal parts water and ginger ale to fill

This drink is often called a "Press" or "VO Press." The latter contains Seagram's VO whiskey, a name brand. If you don't have VO, suggest another blended whiskey as a substitute.

Seven and Seven
1½ oz. Seagram's 7
7-Up to fill
garnish with a lemon

This drink requires name-brand whiskey and the right mixer. If you are missing either ingredient, suggest substitutes. However, be sure to let the drinker know you are substituting ingredients.

POPULAR HIGHBALLS

The popular-drink section contains recipes that are either simple variations of the basics or more complicated, yet often ordered, drinks. If you plan to work at a bar, memorize these recipes. They are arranged by liquor type (and, within these, by variations) to make it easier for you to remember ingredients and proportions.

Vodka and Apple Juice (or Lemonade)

1½ oz. vodka
apple juice (or lemonade) to fill

Hawaiian Seabreeze

1½ oz. vodka
equal amounts of pineapple juice
    and cranberry juice to fill

This drink is delightfully easy to remember if referred to as a "Hawaiian Seabreeze," as it merely substitutes a little touch of Hawaii (pineapple juice) for grapefruit juice in a normal Seabreeze. Unfortunately, local conventions provide for ample possible confusion, as the drink sometimes goes undercover as a "Downeaster" or a "Bay Breeze."

Fuzzy Navel

1 oz. peach schnapps
1 oz. vodka
orange juice to fill
garnish with an orange

Sometimes an extra ounce of peach schnapps is substituted for the vodka.

Sex on the Beach

1½ oz. vodka
1 oz. peach schnapps
cranberry juice to ¾ full
orange juice to fill
garnish with orange or pineapple

Serve with ice in a highball glass.

Sleazy Sex on the Beach

1½ oz. vodka
1 oz. Grand Marnier
cranberry juice to ¾ full
orange juice to fill

Serve with ice in a highball glass.

Moscow Mule

1½ oz. vodka
ginger beer to fill
garnish with a lime wedge

This beverage is traditionally served in a coffee or copper mug.

Mind Eraser

1½ oz. Kahlúa
1½ oz. vodka
soda water to fill

Pour over ice in a highball glass and serve with a straw. Do not shake or stir, since the layering of ingredients is part of the effect. The drinker finishes it off like a shot "down in one" through a straw.

52

Harvey Wallbanger

1½ oz. vodka
orange juice (fill almost to top)
1 oz. Galliano (float on top)

This is a screwdriver with Galliano on top.

Koolaid

1 oz. vodka
1 oz. Southern Comfort
1 oz. amaretto
1 oz. Midori
cranberry juice to fill

Serve with ice in a highball glass.

Purple Haze

1½ oz. vodka
1½ oz. Chambord
1 oz. triple sec
splash of lime juice
soda water to fill

Serve over ice in a highball glass. Like a Mind Eraser, this drink is served in highball glass, but the drinker finishes it off "down in one" through a straw before excusing himself while he kisses the sky.

Bulldog Highball

1½ oz. gin
ginger ale to ¾ fill
orange juice to fill

This is a gin highball with some orange juice in it.

Rum Cape Codder
1½ oz. rum
cranberry juice to fill

Just substitute rum for vodka in a Cape Codder.

Bloody Maria
1½ oz. tequila
tomato juice to ¾ fill
small splash lemon juice (or garnish with a lemon slice/wedge)
dash Worcestershire sauce
dash Tabasco sauce (more for a hotter drink)
shake of salt and pepper
¼ tsp. horseradish (optional)
garnish with a lime or celery stick

Ask if the drinker would like the drink hot, and then adjust the Tabasco accordingly. This drink is a Bloody Mary with tequila instead of vodka.

Mexicola
1½ oz. tequila
cola to fill
garnish with a lime wedge

This is a tequila version of the Cuba Libre. Drinkers call this by other names, such as tequila and cola. However, the reference to Mexico in a drink name generally indicates the presence of tequila.

Tequila Sunrise
1½ oz. tequila
orange juice to fill
splash (½ oz.) of grenadine

Make this like a tequila screwdriver and stir. Then gently add the grenadine on the top of the drink to achieve the "sunrise" look.

Tequila Sunset

1½ oz. clear tequila

dash lime juice

orange juice

½ oz. blackberry brandy (float on top after stirring)

Long Island Iced Tea

1 oz. gin

1 oz. vodka

1 oz. rum

1 oz. tequila

1 oz. triple sec (optional)

splash sour mix

splash Rose's Lime Juice

cola to fill (after stirring)

Iced Teas are very popular these days. If made correctly, they taste like real iced teas (inexplicably, given the actual absence of this ingredient), but feel very different when you find out that all of those lonely ounces can add up to a can of whoop-ass opened on your drunken self. In states with stringent alcohol laws, drinks with 4 oz. of hard alcohol (as in Iced Teas) are prohibited. As a result, bartenders will frequently reduce the presence of each individual alcohol to ½ oz.

Freddy Fudpucker

1½ oz. tequila

orange juice (fill almost to top)

1 oz. Galliano (float on top)

This drink is a tequila version of the Harvey Wallbanger.

SLOES AND SCREWS

The following seven drinks are grouped together to illustrate a helpful technique for drink memorization. They are all modifications of a screwdriver, and while many drinkers will order them solely for the sake of a few sophomoric giggles, a bartender need not be offended by the absurdity of having a patron approach them saying, "I'd like a Sloe Comfortable Screw... please." Instead, savvy servers will content themselves to know that (a) the person ordering the drink will go home lonely, and (b) the drink's name clarifies all of its ingredients. Because so many drinks are simple variations on each other, look for key words in the name of the drink that give away the ingredients. A Sloe Comfortable Screw Up Against the Wall is a complicated drink with many ingredients; however, by dissecting the title, any rookie bartender should be able to make it: Sloe (sloe gin) Comfortable (Southern Comfort) Screw (vodka and orange juice) Up Against the Wall (Galliano – as in Harvey WALLbanger).

Sloe Driver
_____
1½ oz. sloe gin
orange juice to fill

Comfortable Screw
_____
1½ oz. Southern Comfort
orange juice to fill

Sloe Screw
_____
1½ oz. vodka
1 oz. sloe gin
orange juice to fill

Sloe Comfortable Screw
_____
1½ oz. vodka
1 oz. sloe gin
1 oz. Southern Comfort
orange juice to fill

Sloe Comfortable Screw Up Against the Wall

1½ oz. vodka
1 oz. sloe gin
1 oz. Southern Comfort
orange juice (almost to fill)
1 oz. Galliano (float on top)

Screw-Up

1½ oz. vodka
splash orange juice
7-Up, Sprite, or other lemon-lime concoction to fill
garnish with an orange

Mexican Screw

2 oz. tequila
orange juice to fill
garnish with the states of Texas, California, and an orange

FUN HIGHBALLS

You don't have to memorize these drinks because they aren't ordered too often, but keep this book at the bar just in case. They are listed alphabetically for easy reference.

Amaretto, Orange Juice, and Soda

1½ oz. amaretto
equal parts of orange juice and soda to fill
garnish with an orange slice

Bulldog

1 oz. vodka (or rum)
1 oz. Kahlúa
cream to fill
splash of cola on top

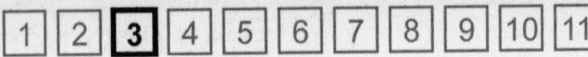

California Root Beer

1½ oz. Kahlúa
1 oz. Galliano
root beer to fill (after stirring Galliano and Kahlúa)

Dark and Stormy

1½ oz. dark rum
ginger beer to fill

This delicious drink is popular in Bermuda, where they use Gosling's rum. If you can't find Gosling's, use another dark or spiced rum.

Gentle Ben

¾ oz. vodka
¾ oz. gin
¾ oz. tequila
orange juice to fill
garnish with a cherry and an orange slice

Kahlúa and Iced Coffee

1½ oz. Kahlúa
iced black coffee to fill

Kahlúa Root Beer Float

1 oz. Kahlúa
1 oz. root beer
dash Galliano
club soda to fill
scoop of vanilla ice cream to top

Do not serve on ice.

Kahlúa, Rum, and Soda

1½ oz. Kahlúa
1 oz. rum
soda water to fill

Lime Rickey

1½ oz. gin
½ oz. Rose's Lime Juice
soda water to fill

Mojito

1½ oz. light rum
1 tsp. sugar
dash Rose's Lime Juice
soda water to fill
garnish with lemon slice and mint

Stir light rum, sugar, and Rose's Lime Juice vigorously with ice before filling with soda water.

Oriental Rug

1 oz. Kahlúa
1 oz. Bailey's Irish Cream
1 oz. Frangelico
1 oz. Jägermeister
cola to fill

Serve over ice in a highball glass. The many swirling colors provide this drink with its name.

Receptacle

1½ oz. vodka
splash each: orange, pineapple, and cranberry juices
top with 7-Up or Sprite
garnish with a cherry and an orange slice

Red Death

½ oz. vodka
½ oz. sloe gin
½ oz. Southern Comfort
½ oz. amaretto
½ oz. triple sec
½ oz. lime juice
½ oz. orange juice
grenadine

Stir and serve over ice. Add enough grenadine for a deep red color. This nasty concoction can also be served as a shot.

Ren and Stimpy

1½ oz. gin
1½ oz. Chambord
cola to fill
garnish with a lime wedge

Serve over ice in a highball glass.

Tequila Dream

1½ oz. tequila
splash cranberry juice
iced tea to fill
garnish with lime

This drink harbors no similarities to the "Tequila Mockingbird" depicted in the shaken section, with the single exception that one disgruntled student (and, arguably, his roommate) thought that in mixing these elements together, he had come up with a tasty concoction deserving of a clever name – namely, that of a "Tequila Mockingbird." Upon discovering that the name had already been taken, his hopes were shattered, leading him to impart a subtle hint of tragedy into his drink's moniker.

Watermelon

1 oz. strawberry liqueur
1 oz. vodka
orange juice to ¾ fill
sour mix to fill
dash grenadine
garnish with an orange slice

Serve over ice in a highball glass.

STIRRED COCKTAILS

The stirred cocktail category includes drinks such as martinis, Manhattans, and gimlets. They are stronger than highballs and measure about 3 oz. of liquid. The exact amount of liquid in the drink depends on the size of the serving glass. Just remember to keep the proportions the same as those listed in these recipes, and don't be afraid to eyeball it if you need to.

You can make stirred cocktails two ways: straight up (or just "up") or on the rocks (or just "rocks"). Straight-up cocktails are made in a shaker glass and then strained into a cocktail glass without ice. On-the-rocks drinks can be made either right in a rocks glass with ice or stirred in a shaker and then strained into a glass with fresh ice. Ask if the drinker prefers a "rocks" or "up" drink, and then:

1. Fill a 12 oz. shaker glass two-thirds full with ice.
2. Put the smallest ingredient in first until all ingredients are in the shaker. It's important to put in the less substantial ingredient first (in the case of a martini, the vermouth) so that you can always adjust in case you pour too much. If you put the gin into a martini before adding too much vermouth, you have to throw the whole drink away. Haste makes waste!
3. Stir well. Very well.
4. Strain the drink into a serving glass.
5. Garnish, if necessary.

The following are basic stirred cocktails. Memorize these classics and practice making them, as martini drinkers are the fussiest people in the world. Be prepared.

MARTINIS

Time to slip out of these wet clothes and into a dry martini.
Mae West

Martinis are one of the more under-appreciated arts of the modem world. Figuring out how to pour in the right amount of vermouth is a struggle even for superstar bartenders. If you are using a metal shaker for your martini – like the pros – some suggest that the ideal way to measure out the vermouth in a martini is by rimming the full edge of the shaker with the stuff. For a dry martini, these experts claim that rimming half of the edge of the shaker will do the trick. For an extra-dry martini, a drinker wants naught but a hint of vermouth in the empty shaker, which amounts to splashing a little bit of vermouth in the empty shaker, swirling it around, and then emptying it out before stirring the gin and ice.

Martini

1 part dry vermouth
5 parts gin
garnish with two olives (pitted and without pimentos)

Pour just a small splash of vermouth (about a one count or a shaker's circumference) in the shaker and then a five count (2½ oz.) of gin. Melted ice will bring the liquid content up to 3 oz.

Dry Martini

1 part dry vermouth
10 parts gin
garnish with two olives (pitted and without pimentos)

Pour a quick dash of vermouth into the shaker (half the shaker's rim) and then add a six count (3 oz.) of gin. With such a high gin to vermouth ratio, it is impossible to eyeball proportions as recommended for other stirred cocktails.

Extra-Dry Martini

splash of vermouth
3 oz. gin
garnish with two olives (pitted and without pimentos)

Splash the vermouth in the bottom of the shaker, swirl it around, and empty the shaker. Fill with ice and pour 3 oz. gin. Stir and strain into martini glass, either straight up or on the rocks (ask the drinker which variant she prefers).

Extra-Extra-Dry Martini

3 oz. gin
garnish with two olives (pitted and without pimentos)

Pour a six count of gin into a shaker filled with ice, strain into a cocktail glass, and make sure that the vermouth bottle doesn't even share a zip code with the gin.

Fifty-Fifty

1½ oz. dry vermouth
1½ oz. gin
garnish with two olives (pitted and without pimentos)

Stir in a shaker and strain into a cocktail glass.

DRY WIT

By now, you've probably noticed that the way to dry out a martini is to reduce the amount of vermouth in the drink. The extra-extra-dry martini is a frequently ordered drink – it sounds a lot more reputable than saying, "Hit me like a punching bag with three cold ounces of gin."

"MARTINIS"

In recent years, as the popularity of martinis has swelled to ridiculous heights not seen since the dream-like days of the "three-martini lunch" (thank you, Jimmy Carter), a number of off-shoot, pseudo-martinis have arisen. Many of these new-fangled drinks have no resemblance at all to actual martinis. Popular wisdom, however, dictates that if you toss the word "martini" into the title of a drink and pour something into a cocktail glass, you can convince the nouveau jet-set to shell out a couple of extra bucks for a very expensive beverage in a "martini bar." Regardless of their suspect relationship with the actual martini family, many of the beverages described here are still delicious.

Gibson

½ oz. dry vermouth
2½ oz. gin
garnish with cocktail onions

Stir in a shaker and strain into a cocktail glass.

Vodka Martini

½ oz. dry vermouth
2½ oz. vodka

Substitute vodka for the gin in a martini.

Tequini or Tequila Martini

½ oz. dry vermouth
2½ oz. tequila

Substitute tequila for the gin in a martini.

Black Martini

1½ oz. vodka or gin
1½ oz. blackberry brandy or black raspberry liqueur

Chocolate Martini

½ oz. crème de cacao
dash orange liqueur (optional)
2 oz. vodka

Cosmopolitan

½ oz. triple sec
½ oz. lime juice
½ oz. cranberry juice
2 oz. vodka
garnish with a lime

French Martini

¾ oz. black raspberry liqueur
¾ oz. peach schnapps
1½ oz. vodka
garnish with a cherry

Saketini

½ oz. sake
2½ oz. gin
garnish with lemon twist or olives (pitted and without pimentos)

MANHATTANS

Manhattans are very similar to martinis in terms of manufacture, but oh so very different in their contents and flavor. Manhattans are generally made with dark alcohols and often use sweet (instead of dry) vermouth.

Manhattan

½ oz. sweet vermouth
2½ oz. blended whiskey
garnish with a cherry

Dry Manhattan

½ oz. dry vermouth
2½ oz. blended whiskey

Perfect Manhattan

1 part (¼ oz.) sweet vermouth
1 part (¼ oz.) dry vermouth
10 parts (2½ oz.) whiskey
garnish with a cherry

You might want to measure these quantities using the rim of the shaker – rim half the shaker with dry vermouth, and the other half with sweet vermouth. Pour in a five count of whiskey, stir, and strain.

Rum Manhattan

½ oz. sweet vermouth
2½ oz. rum
garnish with a cherry

Substitute rum for the blended whiskey in a Manhattan.

Tequila Manhattan
½ oz. sweet vermouth
2½ oz. tequila
garnish with a cherry and a lime wedge

Substitute tequila for the blended whiskey in a Manhattan.

Rob Roy
½ oz. sweet vermouth
2½ oz. Scotch
garnish with a cherry

Substitute Scotch for the blended whiskey in a Manhattan.

Comfort Manhattan
½ oz. sweet vermouth
2½ oz. Southern Comfort
garnish with a cherry

Substitute Southern Comfort for the blended whiskey in a Manhattan.

Latin Manhattan
1 oz. rum
1 oz. dry vermouth
1 oz. sweet vermouth
dash bitters
garnish with a lemon twist

GIMLETS

Gimlet
1 oz. Rose's Lime Juice
2 oz. gin
garnish with a lime wedge

Stir and strain into a cocktail glass.

Vodka Gimlet

1 oz. Rose's Lime Juice
2 oz. vodka
garnish with a lime wedge

Stir and strain into a cocktail glass.

STINGERS

Stinger

1½ oz. brandy
½ oz. crème de menthe

To make a sweet stinger, decrease the amount of brandy and increase the amount of delectable crème de menthe. If a drinker wants to have another form of alcohol substituted for brandy, he or she will specifically ask for a "Vodka Stinger" or a "Scotch Stinger."

STINGERS

To remember that a stinger almost always contains crème de menthe, think of the stinging, cool flavor of the peppermint-flavored alcohol. Alternatively, keep in mind that the brandy bottle often stands next to the crème de menthe on the back bar so that the two may be quickly picked up.

For all practical purposes, the following drinks are members of the stinger family.

Peppermint Pattie

1½ oz. dark crème de cacao
1½ oz. white crème de menthe

Flying Tiger

1 oz. Galliano
1 oz. vodka
1 oz. white crème de menthe

This is a Galliano stinger with vodka.

OLD FASHIONEDS

Old Fashioneds are prepared differently from other stirred cocktails. The following recipe is for the classic Old Fashioned, prepared with whiskey:

1. Put ½ tsp. of fine-grained sugar in the bottom of an Old Fashioned or other lowball glass. That little bump at the bottom of the Old Fashioned glass is there to remind you to do this.
2. Add a dash or two of bitters to the sugar.
3. Put a handful of ice cubes in the glass.
4. Pour in 2½ oz. of whiskey.
5. Add a splash of water or soda water.
6. Stir well. If you use soda water, then switch steps 5 and 6.
7. Garnish with a cherry, an orange slice, and a lemon twist.

Tequila Old Fashioned
½ tsp. fine-grained sugar
1-2 dashes bitters
2½ oz. tequila
splash of water or soda water

Rum Old Fashioned
½ tsp. fine-grained sugar
1-2 dashes bitters
2½ oz. rum
splash of water or soda water

JULEPS

In regions of the southern U.S., the mint julep is as much a religion as it is a drink. Attachment to certain recipes can approximate a form of fanaticism, and a misstep in producing a tasty julep is considered a form of sacrilege (such a mistake can get you killed in Lexington during the weekend of the Kentucky Derby). Con-

sider the childhood (yes, childhood – there are now laws to pre-vent a return of these halcyon days) recollections of William Alexander Percy in his autobiographical *Lanterns on the Levee*, in which he vividly depicts his mother's recipe:

"Certainly her juleps had nothing in common with those hybrid concoctions one buys in bars all over the world under that name. It would have been sacrilege to add lemon, or a slice of orange or of pineapple, or one of those wretched maraschino cherries. First you need excellent bourbon whiskey; rye or Scotch would not do at all… You filled the glass, which apparently had no room left for anything else, with bourbon, the older the better, and grated a bit of nutmeg on the top. The glass immediately frosted and you settled back in your chair for half an hour of sedate cumulative bliss. Although you stirred the sugar at the bottom, it never all melted, therefore at the end of the half hour there was left a delicious mess of ice and mint and whiskey which a small boy was allowed to consume with calm rapture."

Mint Julep
4 sprigs mint
1 tsp. powdered sugar
2 tsp. water
2½ oz. bourbon

In a silver julep cup, silver mug, or Collins glass, grind the mint leaves, sugar, and water together (this can be accomplished by mashing the back of the spoon around the concoction). Fill the glass or mug with crushed ice, then add the bourbon. Top with more ice and garnish with a mint sprig.

Brandy Julep
4 sprigs mint
1 tsp. powdered sugar
2 tsp. water
2½ oz. brandy

Just substitute brandy for bourbon in a Mint Julep.

POPULAR STIRRED COCKTAILS

Although they aren't classics, you'll get many requests for these drinks in a professional bar, so you should memorize them. Now for the good news – drinkers usually prefer these on the rocks, so you can mix them right in the glass (a rocks glass) rather than wasting time transferring them from a shaker glass. The recipes are arranged according to common ingredients and variations, to help you memorize.

Black Russian
1½ oz. vodka
¾ oz. Kahlúa

Mudslide
1 oz. Kahlúa
1 oz. Irish cream
1 oz. vodka

This is very similar to a Black Russian, but it needs to be stirred diligently, since cream tends to resist mixing.

Brave Bull
1½ oz. tequila
1½ oz. Kahlúa

Kahlúa and Amaretto
2 oz. Kahlúa
2 oz. amaretto

Black Watch
1½ oz. Kahlúa
1½ oz. Scotch
splash of soda
garnish with a lemon twist

The Godfather
½ oz. amaretto
1½ oz. Scotch

The Godmother
½ oz. amaretto
1½ oz. vodka

Kamikaze
1 oz. vodka
1 oz. triple sec
1 oz. lime juice

Mix with ice in a metal shaker, then strain into a cocktail or lowball glass.

Rusty Nail
½ oz. Drambuie
1½ oz. Scotch

B and B
1 oz. brandy
1 oz. Benedictine

Stir gently.

Gin Cocktail
2 oz. gin
2 dashes bitters
garnish with a lemon twist

Gin and It
2 oz. gin
1 oz. sweet vermouth

Served neat (no ice used in shaker or cocktail glass).

FUN STIRRED COCKTAILS

You won't get many requests for these drinks, but they're here in case you need them. Recipes here are arranged alphabetically. Most drinks should be prepared with crushed ice in a shaker and then poured into a cocktail glass.

Blanche
½ oz. curaçao
1 oz. anisette
1 oz. triple sec

Beal's Cocktail
½ oz. dry vermouth
½ oz. sweet vermouth
1½ oz. Scotch

Bombay Cocktail
¼ tsp. anisette
½ oz. triple sec
½ oz. dry vermouth
½ oz. sweet vermouth
1 oz. brandy

Dubonnet Cocktail

1½ oz. Dubonnet
1½ oz. gin
garnish with a lemon twist

El Presidente
¾ oz. dry vermouth
1½ oz. light rum
dash bitters

Stir ingredients with ice and strain into a cocktail glass.

Flying Grasshopper

¾ oz. crème de menthe
¾ oz. white crème de cacao
1 oz. vodka

Stir with ice and strain into a cordial glass.

French Breeze

1 oz. peppermint schnapps
2 oz. Pernod

Golden Glow

1 oz. Galliano
1 oz. Drambuie
1 oz. gin

The word "golden" should tip you off as to the presence of Galliano.

Jelly Bean

1 oz. anisette
1 oz. blackberry brandy

Kahlúa and Brandy

1½ oz. Kahlúa
1½ oz. brandy

Negroni

1 oz. gin
1 oz. Campari
1 oz. vermouth (either sweet or dry)
garnish with a lemon twist

St. Patrick's Day

1 oz. crème de menthe
1 oz. Chartreuse
1 oz. Irish whiskey
dash bitters

Sazerac

1 tsp. sugar
dash bitters
dash Pernod
2 oz. bourbon
garnish with a lemon twist

Wandering Minstrel

¾ oz. vodka
¾ oz. Kahlúa
¾ oz. brandy
¾ oz. white crème de menthe

Yale Cocktail

½ oz. dry vermouth
1 tsp. blue curaçao
dash bitters
1½ oz. gin

Those who wish to indulge further in the boorish manner of a Yalie should try either a Bulldog Highball or a Bulldog.

SHAKEN COCKTAILS

This part of bartending is fun and very professional looking once you get the hang of it. When you're starting out, be wary of going overboard and spilling all over yourself and innocent bystanders. (As a precautionary measure, please read "Freestyling" on pg. 73.) Follow the following procedure for all the basic shaken drinks and for all other shaken drinks served straight up. Don't be intimidated by the number of steps; shaken drinks are the easiest drinks to make, as you just have to dump in a few ingredients, give 'em a good shake, and then pour 'em out.

1. Fill the shaker glass two-thirds full with ice.
2. Pour in the ingredients.
3. Put the stainless steel shell over the shaker glass (as shown in the diagram) and press down on the top to make a seal between the two. The steel shell is going to contract when the ice makes it cold, so the seal will get even stronger. That's the magic of science!

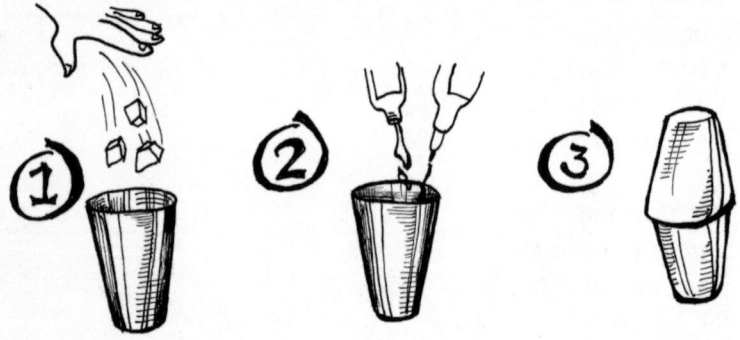

4. Hold the top and bottom of the shaker and shake it up and down. Eventually you can get fancy in your shaking, but always make sure the ingredients go up and down in the glass.
5. You now need to break the seal. A gentle tap either against the heel of your hand or a surface should do. If the seal makes a loud snap as it breaks, don't be alarmed! Your drink is just breaking the tastiness barrier.

6. Keeping the shaker glass and shell together, turn the whole thing over. Then take the glass out of the steel shell. By turning the shaker over so that the shell is on the bottom, you avoid making a mess.

7. Strain the drink from the shell into some type of a lowball glass (preferably one with a stem so that the drink will stay colder longer). The strainer should fit comfortably over the mouth of the shaker to prevent ice from entering the cocktail glass. Pour slowly so that the alcohol doesn't spill all over you.

8. Garnish the drink as necessary.

9. Clean the shaker: pour in some water, shake it around, dump it out, and then wipe the inside. Some shaken cocktails have milk or cream in them, in which case, take special pains in cleaning the shaker – nobody likes a whiskey sour garnished with chunks of curdled milk.

The recipes in the first two sections are arranged in groups of similar drinks to facilitate their mastery. You may find these recipes easy to remember before forging ahead into the real world only to encounter a new problem – you've memorized ingredients and proportions, but you forgot whether to shake or stir. For shame! As a general rule, shake fruit juice, sour mix, sugar, egg, and cream drinks, or drinks that contain other difficult-to-mix ingredients. Some of the multi-liqueur drinks in the stirred section might actually mix better when shaken.

Many of these recipes call for sour mix, a concoction made with juice from one-half lemon and a teaspoon of sugar. This ratio may be adjusted to your personal preference (or to the pre-fabbed bottle of sour mix that you buy), but it is a good idea always to have a bottle of sour mix on hand when tending bar; it will save you a lot of time when making shaken drinks.

BASIC SHAKEN COCKTAILS

SOURS

Whiskey Sour

2 oz. whiskey
1 oz. sour mix
garnish with a cherry and an orange slice

The basic recipe for sours is often varied slightly to create a number of similar beverages: amaretto sours, rum sours, tequila sours, and vodka sours.

Ward Eight

2 oz. whiskey
1 oz. sour mix
½ oz. grenadine
garnish with a cherry and an orange slice

Sour Ball

1 oz. vodka

1 oz. apricot brandy

½ oz. sour mix

½ oz. orange juice

garnish with a cherry and an orange slice

DAIQUIRIS AND VARIATIONS

Daiquiri

2 oz. rum

juice of ½ lime

1 tsp. sugar

A daiquiri uses lime juice, not lemon, so avoid using sour mix in it. Some bars stock a pre-mixed lime and sugar mixture (such as Quik-Lime), but it is not very common. In a crowded, busy bar, some bartenders make daiquiris with sour mix (like a rum sour) and then squeeze a couple of lime wedges on top to fool the customer's taste buds.

Mai Tai

2 oz. rum

½ oz. curaçao

½ oz. orgeat (almond syrup)

¾ oz. lime juice

garnish with a sprig of mint or pineapple and cherry

Shake vigorously before adding a sprig of mint. Alternatively garnish with pineapple and cherry. If you choose the latter path, you might as well stick an umbrella into the crowded drink to complete the tropical feel.

MAI TAIS

Vic Bergeron, known to friends and pirates as Trader Vic, is credited with the invention of the Mai Tai in 1944. He claims to have created the multifarious drink by mixing a 17-year-old rum with hints of orange curaçao flavoring, a touch of orgeat to create an almond residue, some lime, and rock candy syrup (rarely carried in the modem bar). While a wayfaring nomad named Don the Beachcomber claims that he patented the beverage, one is hard pressed to dispute the insistence of the late Trader Vic. Quoth Vic (shortly before his death): "I originated the Mai Tai. Many others have claimed credit. All this aggravates my ulcer completely. Anyone who says I didn't create this drink is a dirty stinker."

Bacardi Cocktail

2 oz. Bacardi rum
1 oz. lime juice
1 tsp. grenadine

MARGARITAS

Margarita

2 oz. tequila
½ oz. triple sec
juice of ½ lime

Shake and strain into a salt-rimmed cocktail or champagne glass. If you've forgotten how to create this salty effect, refer to "Salting Edges" (pg. 46).

COLLINSES

Tom Collins

2 oz. gin
1 oz. sour mix
splash of soda water
garnish with a cherry and an orange slice

Shake, strain into a Collins glass, and then top with a splash of soda water. Note that the main difference between sours and Collinses is the addition of soda water. Also, the sour is usually served without ice in a sour glass, whereas the Collins goes over ice into a highball-like, frosted Collins glass. The Vodka Collins, Rum Collins, and Tequila Collins are all fairly self-explanatory alterations to the original Tom Collins recipe. Just substitute the named alcohol for the gin in a Tom Collins.

John Collins

2 oz. gin
1 oz. sour mix
splash of soda water
garnish with a cherry and an orange slice

Shake, strain into a Collins glass, and then top with a splash of soda water.

Sloe Gin Fizz

2 oz. sloe gin
1 oz. sour mix
soda water to fill

Singapore Sling

1½ oz. gin
¾ oz. wild cherry brandy
1 oz. sour mix
splash of soda water

Shake, strain into a Collins glass, and then top with soda water.

POPULAR SHAKEN DRINKS

Some of these drinks have become so popular in recent years that they're practically basics, so do memorize them if you plan to work in a bar someday. If you tend bar in a busy place, the whole shaker routine may become tiresome and begin to slow you down. To gain a little extra speed, use a half-shell shaker to short-shake drinks on the rocks. This gadget is a small usually plastic shaker shell that fits over regular rocks and highball glasses. If you're using disposable plastic glasses, mix the drink in a highball glass and use a lowball glass for the half shell. Here are the steps for short-shaking (on the following page):

1. Pour the drink ingredients over ice in the appropriate glass.
2. Fit the short-shaker securely over the glass.
3. Shake up and down a few times.
4. Remove the shaker.

Quick and simple! This method is not as neat and thorough as the regular shaker technique, and cannot be used for straight-up cocktails, but it saves valuable time when you're in a hurry.

This section groups drinks with similar ingredients together in hopes of assisting in the process of their memorization.

Gin Fizz
½ tsp. sugar
1½ oz. gin
1 oz. sour mix
dash lime juice
soda water to fill (after shaking all other contents)
garnish with a cherry

Orange Blossom
1½ oz. gin
1 oz. orange juice
¼ tbsp. powdered sugar
garnish with an orange

Shake with ice and strain into cocktail glass.

Gin Daisy
2 oz. gin
1 oz. lemon juice or sour mix
1 tsp. grenadine
1 tsp. sugar
soda water to fill (after shaking all other contents)
garnish with an orange slice

Sombrero

1½ oz. coffee brandy
milk or cream to fill

Serve over ice in a rocks glass. Some bartenders prefer not to shake their Sombreros, the idea being that the cream floats on top like a hat.

Kahlúa Sombrero

1½ oz. Kahlúa
milk or cream to fill

Italian Sombrero

1½ oz. amaretto
milk or cream to fill

White Russian

2 oz. vodka
1 oz. Kahlúa or coffee brandy
½ oz. cream

Serve in a rocks glass. This drink, without the cream, is a Black Russian (a stirred drink).

Dirty Bird

An unstirred, unshaken white Russian

Iguana

½ oz. vodka
½ oz. tequila
½ oz. Kahlúa
1½ oz. sour mix (optional)
garnish with a lime

Shake all ingredients together and then strain into a cocktail glass.

Toasted Almond

1½ oz. Kahlúa or coffee brandy
1½ oz. amaretto
milk or cream to fill

Serve over ice in a rocks or highball glass.

Roasted Toasted Almond

1½ oz. vodka
1½ oz. Kahlúa or coffee brandy
1½ oz. amaretto
milk or cream to fill

Orgasm

¾ oz. amaretto
¾ oz. Kahlúa
¾ oz. Bailey's Irish Cream

Shake over ice and strain into a cocktail glass.

Nuts and Berries

1½ oz. Frangelico
1½ oz. Chambord
milk or cream to fill

Shake and strain into a highball glass.

Girl Scout Cookie

1 oz. vodka
1 oz. coffee liqueur
1 oz. peppermint schnapps
1 oz. cream or milk

Flying Dutchman

2 oz. gin
1 dash triple sec

Creamsicle

1½ oz. amaretto
1½ oz. orange juice
milk or cream to fill

Usually served over ice in a rocks or highball glass. This drink tastes like the ice cream bar of the same name.

Raz-Ma-Tazz

1½ oz. Kahlúa
1½ oz. Chambord
milk or cream to fill

Pink Squirrel

1 oz. crème de noyaux
1 oz. crème de cacao
1 oz. cream

Usually served straight up in a cocktail glass. Memorize these ingredients by remembering that crème de noyaux is red and when mixed with cream it becomes pink. Squirrels eat nuts; crème de noyaux is almond flavored.

Grasshopper

1 oz. green crème de menthe
1 oz. white crème de cacao
1 oz. cream

Serve in a rocks or cocktail glass (usually).

Dirty Grasshopper

1 oz. green crème de menthe
1 oz. Kahlúa
1 oz. milk

Vodka Grasshopper

¾ oz. green crème de menthe
¾ oz. white crème de cacao
¾ oz. vodka
¾ oz. cream

Shake with ice and strain into an Old Fashioned glass over ice.

Alexander

1 oz. gin
1 oz. dark crème de cacao
1 oz. cream or milk

Serve in rocks or cocktail glass.

Alexander's Sister

1 oz. gin
1 oz. green crème de menthe
1 oz. cream or milk

This is also sometimes referred to as a Susanna.

Brandy Alexander

1 oz. brandy
1 oz. dark crème de cacao
1 oz. cream or milk
dash nutmeg on top

Banshee

1 oz. crème de banane
1 oz. white crème de cacao
1 oz. cream

Usually served straight up in a cocktail glass. This drink is similar to a Pink Squirrel, but with crème de banane instead of crème de noyaux. (Banshee and banane are also alliterative!)

Melonball

1½ oz. Midori
¾ oz. vodka
orange juice to fill
garnish with orange

Served over ice in a highball glass.

Apricot Bomb

1½ oz. apricot brandy
2 oz. brandy
1½ oz. triple sec
2 oz. sour mix

Serve over ice in a highball glass.

Cherry Bomb

1½ oz. cherry brandy
2 oz. vodka
1½ oz. triple sec
2 oz. sour mix

Serve over ice in a highball glass.

Scarlett O'Hara

1½ oz. Southern Comfort
1½ oz. cranberry juice
dash lime juice
garnish with lime

Think of Scarlett and remember that scarlet cranberry juice gives the drink its red color. Scarlett O'Hara of *Gone with the Wind* reminds most people of the South, so it should be easy to remember the Southern Comfort.

Iced Tea

1 oz. vodka
1 oz. gin
1 oz. tequila
1 oz. triple sec
splash of lemon juice
cola (to fill after shaking and straining all other contents)

Shake vodka, gin, tequila, triple sec, and lemon juice. Strain into a highball glass over fresh ice before filling with cola.

Zombie

¾ oz. light rum
¾ oz. dark rum
1½ oz. Jamaican rum
2 oz. pineapple juice
1 oz. lime juice
1 oz. orange juice
garnish with a pineapple slice or chunk and a cherry

Shake and strain into a highball glass over fresh ice. Float on top ½ oz. of 151-proof rum. Serve with straws.

Zombie (Variation)

1 oz. light rum
½ oz. Jamaican rum
½ oz. crème de noyaux
½ oz. triple sec
1 oz. lime juice
1 oz. orange juice
soda water
garnish with a pineapple slice or chunk and a cherry

Shake the rums, crème de noyaux, triple sec, and juices. Strain into a highball glass over fresh ice before filling with soda water.

There are limitless numbers of variations on the Zombie. The common denominator to all recipes, however, is that they include as many different kinds of rum as possible while obscuring the taste of the alcohol to the greatest possible degree, thereby turning a reveling drinker into a member of the walking dead.

Comfortable Pirate

1½ oz. Captain Morgan's spiced rum
1 oz. Southern Comfort
pineapple juice to fill
garnish with a member of the Village People

Shake and strain into a highball glass over fresh ice.

Alabama Slammer

¾ oz. Southern Comfort
¾ oz. vodka
¾ oz. amaretto
dash grenadine
splash orange juice

Serve in a highball, cocktail, or shot glass. For a slightly stronger drink, substitute sloe gin for grenadine. Be sure to ask if the drinker wants a highball or a shot and then vary the amounts of the ingredients accordingly, maintaining an equal ratio between the Southern Comfort and the vodka.

Pearl Harbor

2 oz. Midori
1 oz. vodka
pineapple juice to fill
garnish with cherry and pineapple

Serve over ice in a highball glass.

PLANTER'S PUNCH

At first glance, these recipes appear to be difficult to remember. But it's easy to cheat if you have a bottle of Myers's rum – you'll find a recipe printed right on the label!

Planter's Punch

2 oz. rum
1 oz. Myers's rum (Jamaican)
1 tsp. sugar
juice of 1 lime
equal parts orange and pineapple juice to fill
    soda water
garnish with an orange slice and a cherry

Shake rum, Myers's rum, sugar, lime juice, and juices. Strain into a highball glass over fresh ice before topping with soda water.

Planter's Punch (Variation)

2 oz. rum
1 oz. sour mix
splash orange juice
splash pineapple juice
½ oz. Myers's rum (Jamaican)
½ oz. curaçao
garnish with an orange slice and a cherry

Instead of topping with soda water, swirl Myers's rum and curaçao on top. Serve with a straw. The liquors on top give the drink "punch" when sipped through a straw. The drinker finishes the bottom part first and gets an extra boost from the rum and curaçao at the end.

Eggnog

1 egg
1 tsp. sugar
1½ oz. liquor (brandy, whiskey, rum, or a combination)
4 oz. milk
dust of nutmeg on top

Shake with ice and strain into a highball glass without ice. Goes great with Wheaties for that extra-special breakfast of champions. For an extra-foamy nog, try mixing in a blender.

FUN SHAKEN COCKTAILS

Included below is a list of other shaken cocktails which are fun to make (and to drink). Just glance through these drinks to see if they sound good, but don't worry about memorizing them. They are listed alphabetically for easy reference.

Between the Sheets

1 oz. brandy
1 oz. triple sec
1 oz. rum
dash lemon juice or sour mix

Shake and strain into a cocktail mixer.

Bullshot

1½ oz. vodka
4 oz. beef bouillon
dash Worcestershire sauce
dash salt and pepper (optional)
garnish with a lemon twist

Shake with ice and strain into a high-ball glass with ice.

California Lemonade

2 oz. blended whiskey
1 oz. sour mix
juice of 1 lime
dash grenadine
soda water to fill (after shaking all other contents)
garnish with an orange slice, a lemon twist, and a cherry.

Shake whiskey, sour mix, lime juice, and grenadine. Strain into a Collins glass over fresh ice before filling with soda water.

Cherry Rum

1½ oz. rum
½ oz. cherry brandy
½ oz. cream

Shake well and strain into a cocktail glass over ice.

Chocolate Mint Rum

1 oz. rum
½ oz. dark crème de cacao
1 oz. white crème de menthe
½ oz. cream

Shake well and strain into a cocktail glass.

Chuckie

1½ oz. vodka
dash curaçao
splash pineapple juice
splash orange juice
soda water on top (after shaking all other contents)
garnish with a cherry

Shake vodka, curaçao, and juices. Strain into a rocks glass over fresh ice before topping with soda water.

Cream Puff

2 oz. rum
1 oz. cream
1 tsp. sugar

Shake and strain into a highball glass over fresh ice.

Creamy Mocha Mint

¾ oz. Kahlúa or coffee brandy
¾ oz. white crème de cacao
¾ oz. white crème de menthe
¾ oz. cream

Shake and strain into a rocks glass over fresh ice.

Crimson Cocktail

1½ oz. gin
2 tsp. lemon juice
1 tsp. grenadine
¾ oz. port (float on top after shaking all other contents)

Shake the gin, lemon juice, and grenadine, strain into a cocktail glass, and float port on top. Hold sway while drinking!

Cuban Special

1 oz. rum
dash triple sec
splash pineapple juice
juice of ½ lime
garnish with a cherry

Shake and strain into a rocks glass over fresh ice.

Dirty Mother

1½ oz. Kahlúa or coffee brandy
1½ oz. brandy

Shake and strain into a rocks or highball glass over fresh ice. For a slight variation, one can add 1 oz. of cream. Some people refer to this as a Dirty White Mother.

El Presidente Herminio

1½ oz. rum

½ oz. crème de banane

½ oz. curaçao

splash orange juice

splash pineapple juice

Shake and strain into a lowball glass over fresh ice.

Fan

2 oz. Scotch

1 oz. triple sec or Cointreau

1 oz. grapefruit juice

Shake and strain into a rocks glass over fresh ice.

Georgia Cream

1 oz. peach brandy

1 oz. white crème de cacao

1 oz. cream

Shake and strain into a rocks glass over fresh ice.

Golden Apple

1 oz. Galliano

½ oz. applejack

½ oz. white crème de cacao

Shake and strain into a champagne glass rimmed with maraschino cherry juice and dipped in coconut powder (done like salting the rim).

Golden Dream

1 oz. Galliano
½ oz. triple sec or Cointreau
½ oz. cream
½ oz. orange juice

Shake and strain into a cocktail glass or a rocks glass over fresh ice.

Guana Grabber

1 oz. light rum
1 oz. dark rum
1 oz coconut rum (such as Malibu or Cocoribe)
3 oz. pineapple juice
1 oz. grapefruit juice
dash grenadine

Shake and strain into a rocks glass over fresh ice.

Harvard

1½ oz. five-star brandy
½ oz. sweet vermouth
1 dash bitters
1 tsp. grenadine
juice of ½ lemon
garnish with a lemon twist

Shake and strain into a cocktail glass. A fair drink, to be sure, but as fair as Harvard?

Hawaiian

2 oz. gin
1 tbsp. pineapple juice
½ oz. triple sec

Shake with ice and strain into a cocktail glass.

Hot Pants
1½ oz. tequila
½ oz. peppermint schnapps
1 tbsp. grapefruit juice
1 tsp. powdered sugar

Shake with ice and pour into a rocks glass rimmed with salt. Drink while wearing short shorts.

Jack Rosé
2 oz. applejack
juice of ½ lemon
1 tsp. grenadine
garnish with a lemon

Shake and strain into a rocks glass over fresh ice.

Jamaican Cream
1 oz. Jamaican rum
1 oz. triple sec
1 oz. cream

Shake and strain into a rocks glass over fresh ice.

James Bond
"A vodka martini, shaken, not stirred." (However, Bond once ordered bourbon, no ice.)

Mexicana
1½ oz. tequila
1 oz. lemon juice
dash grenadine
1 tbsp. pineapple juice

Shake with ice and strain into a cocktail glass.

Mocha Cream

1 oz. Kahlúa or coffee brandy
1 oz. white crème de cacao
1 oz. cream

Shake and strain into a rocks glass over fresh ice.

Mocha Mint

¾ oz. coffee liqueur or coffee brandy
¾ oz. white crème de menthe
¾ oz. white crème de cacao

Shake with ice and strain into a cocktail glass.

Pink Lady

2 oz. gin
1 oz. cream
½ oz grenadine
1 egg white

Shake and strain into a cocktail glass.

Poppy Cocktail

1½ oz. gin
¾ oz. white crème de cacao

Shake and strain into a cocktail glass.

Ramos Fizz

1½ oz. gin
juice of ½ lemon
juice of ½ lime
1½ oz. cream
½ tsp. sugar
1 egg white
1 tsp. orange juice

Shake and strain into a rocks glass over fresh ice. Top with club soda.

Red Russian

1 oz. strawberry liqueur
1 oz. vodka
1 oz. cream

Shake and strain into rocks glass over fresh ice.

Russian Bear

1 oz. vodka
1 oz. dark crème de cacao
1 oz. cream

Shake and strain into a rocks glass over fresh ice.

Sidecar

1 oz. brandy
½ oz. triple sec
juice of ½ lemon

Shake and strain into a cocktail glass.

Spanish Moss

1½ oz. tequila
1 oz. Kahlúa
3 drops of green crème de menthe

Shake tequila and Kahlúa. Strain into a cocktail glass, and then add three drops of green crème de menthe.

Tam-o'-Shanter (Irish Sombrero)

1 oz. Kahlúa or coffee brandy
1 oz. Irish whiskey
milk to fill

Shake with ice in a highball glass.

Tequila Mockingbird

1½ oz. tequila
¾ oz. green crème de menthe
juice of 1 lime
garnish with a lime slice

Shake with ice and strain into cocktail glass.

Tootsie Roll

1½ oz. Kahlúa
1½ oz. dark crème de cacao
orange juice to fill

Shake with ice in a highball glass. When made correctly, this drink tastes like the eponymous candy.

Tropical Gold

1½ oz. rum
½ oz. crème de banane
orange juice to fill
garnish with an orange slice and a pineapple chunk

Shake with ice in a highball glass.

Velvet Kiss

1 oz. gin
½ oz. crème de banane
1 oz. cream
splash pineapple juice
splash grenadine

Shake with ice in a highball glass.

FROZEN DRINKS

Frozen drinks (also called freezes or blended drinks) taste incredibly delicious. Even the most stubborn and steadfast beer or whiskey drinkers have trouble refusing a frosty piña colada on a hot day. To make blender drinks, follow these few simple steps:

1. Use only a heavy-duty blender. Those wheezing household blenders lack the teeth and the courage to successfully cut the ice. Wrap the blender in cellophane to avoid creating a horrible mess.
2. With the motor off, mix the ingredients in the blender. You can either put the liquor into the blender or leave it out. Given the vast number of people who enjoy the virgin alternatives to frozen drinks, however, we recommend pouring the alcohol directly into the serving glass instead of the blender. That way, you don't have to wash the blender before preparing a virgin version of these drinks. Fill the blender about a quarter of the way with ice, and then add the mixers until the ice just starts to float.
3. Put the lid on.
4. Keeping fingers, hair, loose clothing, and small children at a safe distance, hold the lid down with one hand and start the machine on low speed. After the initial mixing, change to high speed until the ingredients are well blended.
5. Pour the mixture over alcohol in the glass. Stir with a straw or spoon to circulate the alcohol throughout the concoction.

The following recipes are divided into five categories to help you memorize the ones you like: Coladas, Daiquiris, Margaritas, Tropical Drinks, and Ice Cream Drinks.

BLENDED INSANITY

Most blenders range from 24 to 48 oz. in capacity. Since a typical highball glass holds about 12 oz., adjust the ingredient amounts to fit your blender while making sure that you maintain the proportions of the original recipe. In most recipes, the blender will be approximately three-quarters full. As with the ingredients, the exact amount of ice will vary, but simply eyeballing the right amount should be sufficient. In general, increasing the amount of ice in the blender will result in a thicker drink.

COLADAS

Piña Colada

2 oz. rum
1 oz. coconut cream (comes in a can at the supermarket or liquor store)
2 oz. pineapple juice
garnish with a cherry and a pineapple chunk

Blend with ice. If you don't want to measure or use the amounts given in this recipe (in other words, if you just want to throw the ingredients in the blender any old way), follow this basic formula of as much rum as you want (2 parts), 1 part coconut cream, and 2 parts pineapple juice.

PACK THE PIÑA PUNCH

If you don't want a sweet piña colada, reduce the amount of coconut cream. For a slushy drink, add more ice. For a special touch, add a splash of grenadine and you'll have pink piñas. For a richer rum flavor, use golden or dark rum as well as light rum.

Midori Colada

2 oz. Midori
1 oz. rum
4 oz. pineapple juice
2 oz. coconut cream
garnish with a cherry, pineapple chunks, or melon ball

Blend with ice.

DAIQUIRIS

Frozen Daiquiri

2 oz. rum
½ oz. triple sec
1½ oz. lime juice
1 tsp. sugar

Blend with ice.

DAIQUIRI

You can adjust the frozen daiquiri recipe for any fruit in the world. If you have a favorite fruit or flavoring, throw it into the blender with some rum, sour mix, and ice. As an optional inclusion, toss in an appropriately flavored liqueur for that special sauce (for instance, Chambord in a raspberry daiquiri).

Banana Daiquiri

2 oz. rum
½ oz. crème de banane (optional)
1 sliced banana
1½ oz. lime juice

Blend with ice.

Peach Daiquiri

2 oz. rum
½ oz. peach schnapps or peach-flavored brandy
½ cup fresh or canned peaches
dash of lime juice

Blend with ice.

Strawberry Daiquiri

2 oz. rum
½ oz. strawberry liqueur
½ cup fresh or frozen strawberries
1 oz. lime juice
1 tsp. sugar

Blend with ice.

MARGARITAS

Margarita

1½ oz. tequila
½ oz. triple sec
1 oz. lime juice
garnish with a lime slice (optional)

Blend with or without ice and serve in a cocktail or champagne glass rimmed with salt. Always salt the rim before mixing your Margarita.

102

Strawberry Margarita

2 oz. tequila
1 oz. triple sec
4 oz. lemon or lime juice
½ cup strawberries, fresh or frozen
1 oz. strawberry liqueur or 2 tsp. sugar
garnish with a fresh strawberry or a lime slice

Blend with ice. Serve in a cocktail or champagne glass.

Midori Margarita

2 oz. tequila
1½ oz. Midori
1½ oz. sour mix

Blend with ice. Serve in a (salted) cocktail or champagne glass.

TROPICAL DRINKS

Scorpion

2 oz. light rum
½ oz. brandy
2 oz. lemon juice
2 oz. orange juice
garnish with a cherry and an orange slice

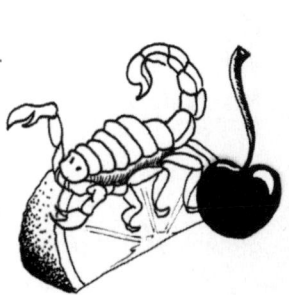

Blend with ice.

Blue Hawaiian

1 oz. light rum
1 oz. blue curaçao
1 oz. cream of coconut
2 oz. pineapple juice
garnish with pineapple

Blend with ice. Consume while wearing Blue Suede Shoes.

Jump Up and Kiss Me

½ oz. Galliano
1½ oz. rum
½ oz. apricot brandy
juice of 1 lemon
1 oz. pineapple juice
½ egg white

Blend with ice. Serve in a brandy snifter.

Golden Cadillac (not really tropical but eh!)

1 oz. Galliano
1 oz. white crème de cacao
1 oz. cream

Combine with a third-cup of crushed ice in a blender at low speed for 10 seconds. Pour into a chilled cocktail or champagne glass.

ICE CREAM DRINKS

Mississippi Mud

1½ oz. Southern Comfort
1½ oz. Kahlúa or coffee brandy
2 scoops of vanilla ice cream
garnish with chocolate shavings

Blend without ice.

Hummer

1 oz. Kahlúa or coffee brandy
1 oz. light rum
2 scoops vanilla ice cream

Blend without ice.

Blended White Russian

1 oz. Kahlúa

2 oz. vodka

2 scoops vanilla ice cream

sprinkle of chocolate shavings

Blend without ice.

SHOTS

It's inevitable – in any bar on a given night, there's going to be a group of folks appearing with a commitment to reliving the splendor of *Animal House*. These people aren't evil, per se, although their titanic appetites for fun can often get the best of them. Before entering into a career of dishing out shots to the irrepressible, it's definitely a good idea to look over Chapter 10 on alcohol safety.

The mechanics of producing shots can range in difficulty from fantastically simple to profoundly baffling. Keep in mind that most people expect their shots chilled (to make them go down more easily). To do this, just fill a metal shaker about a quarter of the way with ice before pouring in the alcohol, then strain the liquor into the shot glasses. The amount of liquor that you want to pour into a shot glass varies between different establishments, generally ranging between 2 and 3 oz.

Since shots are generally consumed in groups, a bartender can simplify his or her job by mastering the art of preparing multiple shots. To do so, follow these simple steps:

1. Line up the glasses for the number of drinks you'll need. This is an especially good idea, since this will prevent you from forgetting how many drinks you're supposed to prepare.

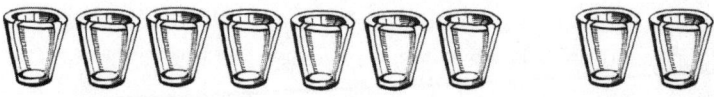

2. Fill a metal shaker half way with ice before pouring in the alcohol. When adding the alcohol, prepare enough booze for one extra drink if more than three drinks have been ordered at once. For reasons that defy explanation, the preparation of shots disproves the scientific logic that matter cannot be destroyed, and you'll often find yourself short of the necessary quantity (especially if you have problems with spillage – an inevitability when preparing lots of shots).

3. Strain equal amounts into each glass. You'll be happy that you prepared too much at this point since you can pour the excess into the glasses to level them off. Generally, you should underpour the first couple of glasses so that you have some liquor with which to top off the needy glasses.

MIXED SHOTS

B-52

½ oz. Grand Marnier
½ oz. Bailey's Irish Cream
½ oz. Kahlúa

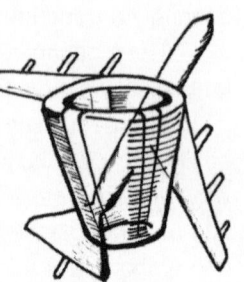

Serve straight up in a shot glass. Some fancy bartenders like to layer these alcohols in reverse order.

Blow Job

½ oz. Bailey's Irish Cream
½ oz. Kahlúa
small glob of whipped cream on top

This is served straight up in a shot glass. The drinker puts his or her mouth entirely over the shot glass and cranes the neck back to drink. No hands allowed! Not in the ever-classy Blow Job. Call your proud parents when you've finished this fine night out.

Brain
¾ oz. Kahlúa
¾ oz. peach schnapps
splash of Bailey's Irish Cream

Do not stir! Usually served straight up in a shot glass. It's the swirling of the Bailey's, which should be added last, that creates the "brain" texture.

Brain Hemorrhage
¾ oz. Kahlúa
¾ oz. peach schnapps
splash of Bailey's Irish Cream
splash of grenadine

Gently pour grenadine on top of a Brain. This is your brain on booze.

Buffalo Sweat
1 oz. bourbon
several dashes Tabasco sauce

Wring the bar rag into the drink. Serve straight up in a shot glass. This drink is a popular "rite-of-passage" drink, especially suitable to 21st birthdays. Occasionally, a customer will ask you to surprise them with something unusual – a Buffalo Sweat will usually do the trick, especially if you're in a vindictive mood. You may opt for something a little less "challenging" if the patron does not resemble a grizzly werewolf.

Cement Mixer
1 oz. Bailey's Irish Cream
1 oz. lime juice

The drinker leans his or her head back and the bartender pours a shot of each ingredient into the open mouth. The swirling effect of

the ingredients (which results in a shockingly pleasant congealing process) coupled with its unusual method of consumption gives this drink its name.

Dead Nazi

1 oz. Jägermeister
1 oz. peppermint schnapps

Serve straight up in a shot glass. The liquors should be cold.

Fireball

1 oz. cinnamon schnapps
dash Tabasco sauce

Serve straight up in a shot glass.

Grape Crush

¾ oz. vodka
¾ oz. Chambord
splash sour mix

Shake with ice and strain into a shot glass.

Hurricane

¾ oz. Jägermeister
¾ oz. Yukon Jack
splash of Bailey's Irish Cream

Do not shake or stir this shot. The Bailey's will create a stormy effect that makes the Dark and Stormy look like a "Sunny Day/ Chasin' the clouds away,/ On my way to where the air is sweet/ Can you tell me how to get,/ How to get to Sesame Street?"

Jell-O Shots

12 oz. vodka
12 oz. water
6 oz. Jell-O gelatin mix (any flavor)

Mix 6 oz. of vodka with 6 oz. of water and bring to a boil. Stir in Jell-O gelatin mix. Remove from stove and add remaining 6 oz. of water and 6 oz. of vodka. Let set in refrigerator overnight. The "shots" can be semigelatinous and drinkable or jelled and eaten with a spoon. Remove the mix from the refrigerator earlier if you do not want solidified Jell-O.

The drinker should be aware that, because Jell-O shots are not completely liquid, the alcohol takes slightly longer to be absorbed into the bloodstream, delaying its effect. For more information on the physiology of alcohol absorption see Chapter 10.

Lemon Drop

¾ oz. Absolut Citron
¾ oz. triple sec

Serve straight up in a shot glass. Give the drinker a lemon slice dipped in sugar as a chaser.

Orange Crush

¾ oz. vodka
¾ oz. triple sec
orange juice to fill

Serve straight up in a shot glass.

Prairie Fire

1½ oz. tequila
Tabasco sauce to fill

Serve straight up in a shot glass.

Snakebite

1½ oz. Yukon Jack
juice of ½ lime

Serve straight up in a shot glass.

Tequila Popper

1 oz. tequila
1 oz. ginger ale

Cover the shot glass with a napkin and hand, then slam it on the table top. Drink while foaming.

Terminator

½ oz. Jägermeister
½ oz. Bailey's Irish Cream
½ oz. peppermint schnapps
½ oz. bourbon

Serve straight up in a shot glass. Drink enough of these and the contents of your stomach will be threatening, "I'll be back."

Windex

¾ oz. vodka
¾ oz. blue curaçao

Serve straight up in a shot glass.

Woo Woo

¾ oz. vodka
¾ oz. peach schnapps
cranberry juice to fill

Stir and strain into a shot glass.

LAYERED SHOTS

With the exception of floating fruit in Jell-O, perhaps the greatest culinary mystery remains the elegant production of beautiful and distinct layers of alcohol in a shot glass. Layered shots, also known as pousse-cafés, are perhaps the most scientifically demanding of drinks, in addition to being the most time-consuming drinks to prepare. When you pour several liquids carefully into a shot glass, the heaviest ones stay on the bottom and the lightest ones float to the top, thus creating layers. To make these drinks, be careful, and for the love of God, have patience! If you pour too quickly, your alcohol won't float, and your masterpiece will be destroyed. The following steps provide the appropriate protocol for pouring layered shots:

1. Tip the bar spoon upside down and lower it into the glass until it is just resting atop the alcohol and touching the side of the glass.
2. Lower the speedpourer down as close to the back of the bar spoon as humanly possible. Keep your index finger firmly nestled over the air hole on the back of the speedpourer to slow down the rate at which the liquor flows. Always pour the heaviest liquid first, then the next heaviest, and so on.
3. Since you're keeping your finger over the air hole, the three-count technique becomes useless; instead, eyeball the liquid to a height of about a quarter inch. That will roughly approximate 1 oz.
4. Success! Oooh, pretty!

If your task merely consists of "floating" an ingredient, you will need far less precision. Just lower the speedpourer as close as possible to the top of the drink and give it about a splash (a one count). Floated alcohols are invariably less dense than their sunken counterparts and will stay atop their brethren.

The recipes here list the ingredients from heaviest to lightest, so pour them in the given order. Pour just enough of each liquid to get a smooth, flat layer, but feel free to experiment with the proportions listed here to change the thickness of the layers.

Angel's Delight

1 part grenadine
1 part triple sec
1 part Crème Yvette
1 part cream

Angel's Kiss

1 part white crème de cacao
1 part Crème Yvette
1 part brandy
1 part cream

Angel's Tip

1 part dark crème de cacao
1 part cream

Stick a toothpick through a cherry and balance it on top of the glass.

Angel's Wing

1 part white crème de cacao
1 part five-star brandy
1 part cream

Christmas

1 part grenadine
2 parts green crème de menthe

Fifth Avenue

1 part dark crème de cacao
1 part apricot brandy
1 part cream

King Alphonse

1 part brown crème de cacao

2 parts cream

This is an Angel's Tip without the cherry.

King's Cup

2 parts Galliano

1 part cream

Princess

3 parts apricot brandy

1 part cream

Stars and Stripes

1 part grenadine

1 part heavy cream

1 part blue curaçao

MAKE YOUR OWN LAYERED SHOTS

Each liqueur has a specific weight. The key to making pousse-cafés is to put the heaviest liqueur in the glass first, then the next heaviest, and so on. Cream floats on the top. Technically, you could probably layer all of the liqueurs listed here on top of each other, but most layered shots have only three to five layers. The chart included on the next page assigns numbers to the relative weights of the most popular layered-shot ingredients, from heaviest to lightest. Bonne chance!

Liqueur	Relative Weight
Anisette (50 proof)	17.8
Crème de noyaux (50 proof)	17.7
Crème de menthe (60 proof)	15.9
Crème de banane (50 proof)	15.0
Maraschino liqueur (50 proof)	14.9
Coffee liqueur (50 proof)	14.2
Cherry liqueur (48 proof)	12.7
Parfait Amour (50 proof)	12.7
Blue curaçao (60 proof)	11.7
Blackberry liqueur (50 proof)	11.2
Apricot liqueur (58 proof)	10.0
Orange curaçao (60 proof)	9.8
Triple sec (60 proof)	9.8
Coffee brandy (70 proof)	9.0
Peach brandy (70 proof)	7.0
Cherry brandy (70 proof)	6.8
Blackberry brandy (70 proof)	6.7
Apricot brandy (70 proof)	6.6
Rock and Rye liqueur (60 proof)	6.5
Ginger brandy (70 proof)	6.1
Peppermint schnapps (60 proof)	5.2
Kümmel (78 proof)	4.2
Peach liqueur (60 proof)	4.1
Sloe gin (60 proof)	4.0

CHAPTER 4:
THE WORLD OF BEER

When man first learned to ferment grain into beer more than 10,000 years ago, it became one of his most important (and enjoyable) sources of nutrition. Now, beer has become so much more than a beverage quaffed by primitive cave-dwellers — although after talking to some of the people you'd encounter at a typical college frat party, you may think otherwise. With the increasing popularity of imported beer and the enhanced quality of domestic brands, beer is fast becoming a gourmet beverage. That said, you may have to wait a while before you can pair *fois gras* and truffles with your favorite pilsner.

The many different styles and flavors of beer offer countless options to the aficionado and casual drinker alike. We've moved beyond "Beast" and "Bud," to the exotic realm of Tsingtao, Guinness, Lowenbrau, and Beast Light. Hey, sometimes there's nothing wrong with fine-tuning a classic.

A BRIEF HISTORY OF BEER

Beer is an alcoholic beverage that is fermented and brewed from rice, barley, corn, hops, water, and yeast. The oldest alcoholic beverage known to man, beer has been credited with being the cornerstone of civilization itself—and should it come as any surprise? Something had to keep those cavemen warm when they went off hunting woolly mammoths or their future spouses. It has even been recorded that in some ancient cultures, beer was so valuable that it was sometimes used to pay workers as part of their daily wages. This might put the Tower of Pisa into context.

Like the Pilgrims, Christianity, and smallpox, beer also enjoyed the distinction of coming to the Americas on the Mayflower. In fact, the Pilgrims decided to land at Plymouth Rock instead of Virginia because their beer supply had been completely exhausted. The weary (and sober) Pilgrims landed ashore and encountered a lone

Native American who approached them and said, in perfect English:

"Welcome, English. I am Samoset. Do you have beer?"

The Pilgrims were sure this was a sign from God. Later, Samoset explained that he had learned English – and the fact that ships approaching the coastline frequently carried delicious beer—from coming into contact with English fishing vessels. After receiving some much-needed help from the Native Americans, the Pilgrims celebrated the first Thanksgiving that following November over plates of maize and turkey and frothy mugs of beer.

Today, thousands of varieties of beer are enjoyed throughout the world. The United States alone has over 900 microbrews (made by small, independent brewers). But that's nothing compared to Germany, which at last count has over 1,200 breweries.

Beers come in all shapes and sizes.

BEER: A TRADITION

4,000 years ago, in Babylon, it was a custom that, for a month after a wedding, the bride's father would provide his new son-in-law with all of the mead or beer he could drink. The month following the wedding was called the "honey month" which eventually evolved into the word "honeymoon." Mead is made from honey and there continues to be no better way to celebrate a honeymoon than consuming massive amounts of beer. If your kids ask why you look so funny in your wedding pictures, tell 'em that it's *tradition*.

Beer was primarily shipped and sold in barrels and glass bottles until 1935, the year the first aluminum beer car was introduced to America in a joint effort by American Can Company and Kreuger Brewing. Although beer is most commonly found in cans today, more upscale brands and microbrews are usually found in glass bottles. These bottles are also the primary reason that one should never walk barefoot around upscale college campuses.

BREWING BEER

The beer brewing process begins with a dream. A dream involving hundreds of pounds of pure water, corn grits, and barley. Brewing beer is a step-by-step process.

1. **MALT PREPARATION**: The brewer steeps the barley in water and heats it to begin the beer-making process. This step imparts color and taste to the beer; depending on the degree of roasting, the final product will be pale and light or dark and robust. The product, malted barley ("malt") is often nicknamed the "soul of beer."

2. **MASHING**: Mashing involves a rather complicated process for preparing the malted barley. The malt enzymes break down the starch to sugar and the complex protein of the malt to simpler nitrogen compounds.

3. **LAUTERING**: The brewer removes spent grains and continues brewing the liquid. The spent grains are either discarded or sold as livestock feed.

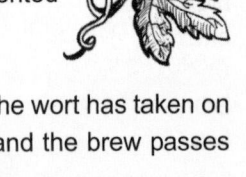

4. **BOILING & HOPPING**: The liquid is transferred to the brew kettles, where it's boiled and hops are added. Hops, the dried flower cones of the hop vine, give beer a sharp, bitter kick and balance out the sweetness of the malt sugars. Hops also contribute a pleasant aroma to the brew and help to preserve freshness. This unfermented mixture of malt and hops is called wort.

5. **HOPS SEPARATION & COOLING**: After the wort has taken on the flavor of the hops, they are removed and the brew passes through a cooling device.

6. **FERMENTATION**: The wort then moves to the wort cooler, where it is left to settle. Yeast (which converts sugar into alcohol and carbon dioxide) and sterile air are added to the wort and the

resulting mixture is poured into fermentation tanks for a carefully controlled time
period.

7. **STORAGE**: After fermentation, the beer
is cooled and placed in storage for at least
two to four weeks.

8. **PACKAGING**: The beer is then bottled or
canned. Before sealing the containers, the
beer passes through a pasteurizer where
its temperature is raised as high as 140 degrees to kill the yeast, then cooled to room
temperature. The bottles are then capped
and sold to customers around the world.

YEAST

Two different types of
yeast can be used in a
brew: **BOTTOM** and **TOP**.

BOTTOM YEAST settles
to the bottom of the tank
after converting all the
sugar to alcohol (the re-
sulting beer is known as
a *lager*).

TOP YEAST rises to the
top of the tank when it's
done converting the
sugar (the resulting beer
is known as an *ale* and
has a stronger flavor than
lager).

BEER VOCABULARY

ALE is top-fermented beer brewed at higher temperatures (around
140°F). Sometimes known for its distinct fruitiness, ale tastes
hoppier (more bitter) than lager and has a higher alcohol content
(4.4% to 5.5% as opposed to lager's 3.2% to 4.5%). Popular ales
include Molson Golden, Ballantine, and Bass.

BITTER BEER is a strong ale, usually English in origin, with a
higher than normal alcohol content and, as the name suggests, a
bittersweet taste.

BOCK BEER (such as **GENESEE BOCK**) is an amber-to-dark-
colored lager beer containing 3.5% alcohol. It is brewed from
caramelized malt and has a strong, sweet taste.

ICE BEER is brewed in the usual manner, then chilled to around
25°F. Some of the water in the brew turns to ice crystals, but the
alcohol, which has a lower freezing point, does not. The crystals

are filtered out, leaving a smoother tasting beer with a slightly higher alcohol content (around 5.6%).

LAGER is a bottom-fermented beer brewed at relatively low temperatures (around 131°F) for a long period of time. The word lager is German for "to store." Most popular, mass-produced American beers are lagers.

LAMBIC BEER is brewed in tiny quantities immediately south of the Belgian capital, Brussels. Ingredients such as raspberries, cherries, caramel, sugar, molasses, and wheat are added during the brewing process to give the beer a unique flavor and sweetness.

LIGHT BEERS

Light beers are extremely popular in America these days, especially among the dieting and health-conscious. Although they contain less alcohol, that's a small price to pay for the amount of calories you save per beer. Some of the offerings available include:

Amstel Light (95 cal)
Budweiser Light Beer
 (108 cal)
Coors Light (110 cal)
Kirin Light (105 cal)
Michelob Light (134 cal)
Miller's Light (96 cal)
Stroh Light (115 cal)

LIGHT BEER has fewer calories than regular beer but one downside: less alcohol.

MALT LIQUOR is a lager that is fermented at a higher temperature than other beers resulting in a higher alcohol content than other lagers (over 5%). It tastes hoppier than beer, but lighter than ale (meaning that it can taste pretty gross).

PILSNER is a light, hoppy, dry lager named for the famous brews of Pilsen in the Czech Republic. As a bartender, you will serve a lot of "light" pilsners (i.e., Miller Lite, Amstel Light), which are brewed with extra enzymes and therefore have lower caloric, carbohydrate, and alcohol contents.

PORTER is an ale with a rich, heavy foam. It has a slightly less hoppy taste than a *stout* and contains 5% to 6% alcohol.

SAKE is beer brewed and processed from rice and water. (Some consider sake a wine.) The alcohol content of sake is about 10-20% and it can be served warm or at room temperature.

120

STOUT is a sweet, dark brown ale produced from heavily roasted barley. It has a thick texture, a slightly bitter flavor, and contains 5% to 6% alcohol.

TRAPPIST BEER is brewed in Belgium or the Netherlands by monks characterized by their austerity and vows of silence. This beer is dark in color and contains high levels of alcohol—a factor that might make silence even scarcer than beer-brewing monks.

WHEAT BEER is made…you guessed it…with wheat. It is usually served with a lemon garnish and sometimes a bit of raspberry syrup.

BEER BRANDS

With so many types of beers out there to choose from, the average beer drinker has literally hundreds of different ways to enjoy a frothy beer at the end, middle, or beginning of the day. Do you prefer a light-tasting low-calorie beer, or a gut-busting fuller-bodied brew? Does the familiar taste of Budweiser or Miller take you back to the ballpark? Will a Corona or Dos Equis deliver you from your cold, New England apartment to a balmy tropical beach just south of the equator? Maybe the Guinness you just poured yourself will whisk you off to the hills of Ireland, where you're fighting off an angry leprechaun with your shillelagh. Whatever choice you make, exploring your options can be a lot of fun.

YE OLDE STANDARDS

There are several no-frills brews that you'll see at most college parties and sporting events. Each has its own claim to fame, whether it's a claim of royalty, presidency, or just a sudden increase in attractive women surrounding the premises. **COORS**, **MILLER**, and **BUDWEISER** all offer both regular and light beer varieties that taste remarkably similar to one another. All go down

easy, though some complain this is because they are too watery. Still, their nationwide availability and party appeal keep these brews at the top of the American beer market.

DOMESTIC BREWS

Because of some stiff competition from foreign breweries, the quality of domestic beers is steadily rising, putting new regional breweries and microbreweries on the beer-brewing map. These varieties of region-specific beers offer a real advantage for beer drinkers, and not just because they now have more brands to experiment with. Because many of these small, independent breweries produce their product in relatively small amounts to limited geographic areas of the country, their beer does not have to travel far and is fresher and more flavorful as a result. Among the regional beers currently available:

ANCHOR STEAM, brewed by Anchor Brewing Company in San Francisco, is deep orange in color with a creamy head and slightly sweet, malty taste. A perfect beer for a nice, juicy steak.

LONE STAR BEER, just like rodeo, two-stepping, and the Alamo, has secured its place in Texan culture. A pale yellow brew with a minimal head, Lone Star beer is easy to drink and dirt cheap. A great thirst quencher.

BROOKLYN LAGER is the most well known beer hailing from the Brooklyn Brewery in New York, and is definitely a local favorite as well as a national one to beer aficionados of the U.S. This amber-gold beer has a malt center with floral aromas and a hint of bitterness, and is praised for its near-perfect amount of carbonation.

ROLLING ROCK PREMIUM BEER, now widely available on the East Coast, has become the preferred drink of hip young urbanites and nerdy young urbanites who are just trying to keep up appearances.

REDHOOK EXTRA SPECIAL BITTER ALE, from the Redhook Ale Brewery in Seattle, pours a medium amber color with a nice foamy head and great clarity. It's spicy, not too bitter, and very accessible to the novice beer drinker.

SIERRA NEVADA BROWN ALE, produced by the Sierra Nevada Brewing Company in Chico, California, is a dark brown ale with a mildly sweet and roasted flavor.

SAMUEL ADAMS BOSTON STOCK ALE, from the Boston Beer Company, is clear, light amber and subtly fruity. Their Samuel Adams Boston Lager is also good; it is clear with a fruity scent and a clean, sweet taste. Sam Adams produces great beers for novice and well-seasoned beer drinkers alike.

> **DRY BEERS**
>
> The latest trend is to "dry" beers, which eliminates a lot of the aftertaste commonly associated with beer. Among the more popular beers in this category are BUD DRY, MICHELOB DRY, KIRIN DRY, and SAPPORO DRY.

BEERS FROM AROUND THE WORLD

The sophisticated and well-traveled beer drinker (aka, town drunk) knows that more and more imports are appearing on the market today. It can be hard to choose, since the style, color, and taste of imported brews can vary as widely as the cultures and cuisines of the countries and regions they belong to. No bar is complete without at least one great imported selection, but you should have no problem selecting a brand you like among the hundreds of foreign beers offered in stores around the country. Here are just a few of the world's most popular imports:

BELGIUM: Stella Artois – this beer's distinctive, full flavor comes from its longer brewing time and use of Bohemian Saas hops; Hoegaarden White – this beer contains both sweet and sour flavors, with a hint of fruit and a slightly bitter aftertaste.

CANADA: Labatt Blue – this pilsner is clean and crisp in flavor with the slightest hint of lemon and a touch of sweetness.

BEER & FOOD

Sure, Tsingtao goes with Chinese. But, in general, how do you select a beer to best complement a certain type of food? The rule for wine can also be applied to beer: ales best complement red meat and lagers best complement white meat. Of course it's always a good idea to experiment, especially with "unconventional" pairings. Who knew, for example, that a rich stout is an excellent complement to a chocolate dessert or that several Beasts make a perfect match for your mother-in-law's meatloaf?

CHINA: Tsingtao – the unique and strong malt flavor makes this beer (conveniently) pair perfectly with Chinese food.

CZECH REPUBLIC: Pilsner Urquell – promoted as the world's first golden beer, Pilsner Urquell boasts the original (and, according to its home brewery, the best) hoppy flavor that came to define the pilsner.

GERMANY: Beck's – this full-bodied lager has a slightly fruity taste and golden color with a dry finish.

GREAT BRITAIN: Bass Pale Ale – the brewers of this beer will be the first to remind you that their beer was enjoyed by Napoleon and Buffalo Bill, and even painted by Manet. Bass Ale has a malty and slightly hoppy taste combined with a full-bodied, burnt roast flavor that makes it a favorite of many in the U.S.; Newcastle Brown Ale – brewed specifically to prevent bitterness, this beer has a hint of caramel and an earthy finish.

HOLLAND: Heineken Lager Beer – a generic-in-taste beer with an amazing website. Forget whatever is written in your bar's bathroom stall and go to www.heinekenexperience.com for a good time; Amstel Lager – with its light version promoted as "the beer drinker's light beer," both versions are light pilsners with some dark malt added to create a uniquely refreshing beer with a slightly bitter taste.

IRELAND: Guinness Draught – when it first hits your mouth, this beer tastes malty with a hint of caramel, and a slightly bitter finish follows.

JAPAN: Sapporo Premium Beer – this light-bodied lager has a crisp tastes that makes it a refreshing choice for accompanying a meal or to drink by itself.

124

MEXICO: Dos Equis XX Special Lager – the makers of this beer describe it as a "golden, aromatic European-style pilsner" with a crisp and refreshing taste; Corona – this smooth and refreshing beer is a favorite of beach bums everywhere because of its light density and the ease with which a bottle of it can be chugged through a lime wedge.

BUZZ CUT: NON-ALCOHOLIC BEER

Non-alcoholic beer. Almost as jarring to look at as the word "sugar-free candy," nonalcoholic beer has turned out to be the wise drink of choice for beer drinkers who enjoy the taste of malt, but need to drive home at night without killing themselves. Beer can lose its alcohol in two ways. The first way is by heating it under a vacuum and distilling out the alcohol. However, this process often alters the distinct flavor of the beer. The second, more costly method, used by Anhauser-Busch in the making of O'Doul's, is a *membrane filtration process* that passes the beer through a membrane that filters out the good from the good: the alcohol is removed, but the flavor of the beer remains. Although there are not very many non-alcoholic beers on the market right now (for obvious reasons), they are slowly making their way into stores nationwide, along with low-carb candy, caffeine-free soda, and the fourth horseman of the apocalypse. The non-alcoholic options that have more flavor tend to be imported. The better brands include: **BUCKLER**, **HAACKE BEST**, **KALIBER** (produced by the Guinness Brewing Company), **MOUSSY**, **WARTECH NONALCOHOLIC BREW**, and **O'DOULS**. Happy drinking, designated drivers!

STORING & SERVING SUGGESTIONS

Unlike many wines and few people, beer does not get better with age—in fact, beer is like that hot girl from your high school who gained 30 pounds and a stomach full of stretch marks after high school. In other words, beer keeps poorly. Bottled beer has a peak life expectancy of only six months, canned beer half that time, and kegs (which are unpasteurized) only one month. Keep this in mind when you see amazing beer sales at the supermarket or liquor store—any time you see a beer priced considerably lower than it ought to be, it's a safe bet that it is past its prime. This does not necessarily mean it's not drinkable; however, you should resist the urge to stock up on huge quantities of beer if you're not going to drink them immediately. Today, most beers have labels giving the day they were brewed or the day they should be removed from the shelf, and this makes it much easier to detect bad beer in advance.

Beer is sensitive to temperature extremes and to light, so store it in a cool dark area—your refrigerator, for example. The ideal temperature is somewhere between 40°F and 60°F. At higher temperatures, the ingredients in beer break down and the aroma and flavor deteriorate, resulting in "skunked beer." When frozen, the solids separate from the liquid and form flakes that do not go back into the solution when the beer thaws.

Just like Baby Bear's porridge, beer shouldn't be served too hot (that's just gross), or too cold (it loses some of its flavor), but just right. As a general rule, most American light-bodied beers are best served at around 42°F, imported beers are best at 47°F to 50°F, and full-bodied ales offer their best flavor at 55°F.

Beer can be served in mugs, goblets, pilsner glasses, plastic cups, or hands depending on the occasion. To serve the perfect beer, start with a sparkling clean glass dipped in cold water. You should keep special glasses just for beer; a film on the glass—from milk or detergent, for example—can alter the taste of the beer. If you like, you can be even swankier and frost

THE "WEIGHT" MYTH

Excess pudge on college students and sports fans is often attributed to the consumption of alcohol, especially beer (hence, "beer belly"). However, beer actually has fewer calories than other liquors. An average bottle contains only 150 calories, and light beers have even less. So, instead of blaming your can of brew for your weight problems, you should probably be shaking your fist at the three shots of vodka you had half an hour ago or the philly cheese steak you're currently stuffing into your mouth.

 your glasses in advance by placing them in your freezer at least an hour before serving. To serve beer—whether from a bottle, can, or tap—pour it slowly into a glass tilted at a forty-five degree angle so the stream of liquid flows down the side and prevents excessive foam (the "head" of the beer) from forming. When the glass is about two-thirds full, pour the beer straight down the middle of the glass until full, leaving a head of about three-fourths of an inch. If you prefer your beer without a head, keep the glass tilted until full.

SERVING BEER: GUIDELINES

For a standard, four-hour cocktail party, plan on about one case of beer (24 beers) for every 10 guests. Keep in mind that younger crowds tend to drink much more beer than older ones, and the quality of beers differs even more widely than that of liquors. If you're having 35 guests or more, consider purchasing a quarter keg (about 7.8 gallons—the equivalent of more than three cases, or 83 12 oz. servings). For 70 guests, buy a keg (technically a half-keg, which contains 15 gallons—about seven cases or 165 12 oz. servings). Keg beer is economical in the long run, but you will have to pay a deposit for the keg and tap. For the best-tasting beer, move the keg to its party location at least four hours before the party and keep it consistently cold until empty. Put it in a big tub or barrel, pack chunks of ice around it (try for block ice, which won't melt as fast as cubed or cocktail ice), and cover it with a big plastic bag or towel to catch the water.

Choosing a beer for your keg can be tricky, and often depends more on your budget than on your taste. For an inexpensive party, especially for younger crowds, a simple keg of light beer such as **BUDWEISER**, **COORS**, or **MILLER** keeps weight watchers happy and keeps everyone from getting beer bloat (that overly full feeling that results from prolonged heavy beer drinking). For classier parties, you may want to try a seasonal beer. **SAM ADAMS** makes both an Octoberfest brew and a **SUMMER ALE** and **HARPOON BREWERY'S WINTER WARMER** is a holiday favorite.

KEG SPECIFICS

Most kegs use a standard pressure-tap. Take hold of the two small outcropping handles attached to the ring at the base and turn counterclockwise. Then place the tap on the outlet and turn the ring clockwise to screw it into the keg. If you didn't turn the ring far enough in the counterclockwise direction, you may find yourself soaked in beer. You can raise the pressure on the stream of beer flowing out by pumping the tap; you can lower the pressure by pulling on the small release pin at the base of the tap. You can lower the pressure of your social surroundings by starting to drink the beer before the party even starts. The first few beers coming out of the keg will usually be very foamy. You will have to pump the tap periodically to keep a steady stream flowing as the level of beer decreases. A very small minority of taps works differently from this one; don't hesitate to ask for more information at the liquor store when you pick up the keg.

CONCLUSION:
DON'T BE A DUD, CRACK OPEN A BUD

Beer is the perfect accompaniment to a sporting match, casual gathering of friends, or raucous college party. So crack open that can, tap that keg, pour out a glass, and savor the unique joys and (sometimes) disastrous consequences of this cool and frothy beverage.

CHAPTER 5:
THE WORLD OF WINE

The trend in wine for the 21st century is to forget the hard-and-fast (aka, snobbish) rules that have long dictated the drinking of wine. Now we can enjoy the wine we like with the foods we like—anytime we like. Those unfamiliar with the many subtleties of wine, and those who are simply not experts, are much less likely to be scared away by arrogant connoisseurs. While there's no longer a stigma attached to simply finding a wine you enjoy and then sticking to it, experimentation is bound to lead to some wonderful new discoveries.

As you begin to try different wines, remember which wines you didn't like and, most importantly, those you especially enjoyed. Wine appreciation is entirely subjective, and once you know what you like, you'll be able to choose accordingly in almost any situation. The most basic guideline, to help get you on the right track, is that lighter wines best complement lighter foods, and fuller-bodied wines go with heavier foods.

Prices are not always the best indicators of quality—it's entirely possible to find a $7 bottle (or box, for that matter) of wine that you like just as much as one that costs 10 or even 20 times that amount. To find a good wine at a reasonable price, look for sales and ask wine store clerks for advice whenever you have questions.

IT'S NO SECRET

Scientific studies have shown that birds and primates are drawn to the smell of ethanol made by fermenting fruits. It's quite possible, then, that wine was already waiting for humans when we came on the scene.

TYPES OF WINE

The three basic kinds of wine are red, white, and rosé. Interestingly enough, the color does not indicate the color of the grapes from whence they came, but instead the length of time that the grape skins stay in the wine during fermentation. Wines are further classified as still, sparkling, or fortified. Still wines are non-carbonated beverages containing 7-15% alcohol. Sparkling wines, such as champagne, sparkling burgundy, and Asti Spumante, are all bubbly and may be any of the three colors and contain anywhere from 7-15% alcohol. Fortified wines, such as port and sherry, contain brandy, which brings the alcohol content up to a heftier 18-22%.

Wine is made all over the world in an ever increasing number of countries. Within most of these countries are a large variety of wine-producing regions, and wines frequently take their name from the region in which they're produced. For example, Chablis is a white wine from the Chablis region in France, while burgundy is a red wine conveniently from the Burgundy region. Wine makers will occasionally take liberties with these designations—many American wines are known as Chablis despite that fact that they are produced in the United States.

AGED TO PERFECTION

The oldest bottle of wine to date was found in Speyer, Germany, inside of one of two sarcophagi unearthed during an excavation. The bottle is dated around 325 AD. In addition to the remnants of wine, the bottle also contained what is most likely olive oil, used more frequently than corks at the time. The olive oil was poured on top of the wine, forming a layer between the wine and the air above.

FRENCH WINES

These are named for the region they are grown in. For example, if you pick up two bottles of white Burgundy, one might say Meursault and one might be a Macon-Villages. They are both made from the Chardonnay grape, but they come from different areas in Burgundy. The following are the general categories of wine produced in France:

RED WINES

RED BORDEAUX: Made from a mix of three grapes, usually Cabernet Sauvignon, Merlot, and a Cabernet Franc. Their general flavor characteristics are cassis and cherry, sometimes eucalyptus, woody, or cedarlike, and some even have a tobacco flavor.

Commonly served with simply roasted meats or fowl. Good with mushrooms, cheese dishes, and other medium to full-flavored dishes.

RED BURGUNDY: Made from the pinot noir grape. Characteristically less tannic, softer and fruitier than Bordeaux, emphasizing fruit flavors such as strawberries and boysenberries; jammy, plummy, and woody are other possible descriptions. Good with roasted meats and lighter dishes such as fish. Also good with cheeses and other earthy foods.

RHONE WINES: Made from a mix of many different grapes, depending on the region. The most common is the syrah grape. Some Rhone wines contain up to twenty different kinds of grapes. They are typically bigger, heavier, full-bodied wines; tannic with a higher alcohol content. Other characteristics are pepperiness, cherry flavor, spiciness, jamminess, and fruitiness. Goes well with heavily spiced, full-flavored foods, such as barbecue, spicy pasta dishes, sausages, and stews.

BEAUJOLAIS: Made from the gamay grape. There are two types of Beaujolais. The first, Beaujolais Nouveau, receives a lot of attention each November when it's released. It is shipped almost immediately after bottling and is very light, fresh, and fruity and contains very little acidity. It's an easy wine for beginning wine drinkers to like. The other, referred to simply as Beaujolais, or "Cru Beaujolais," has a bit more body, acid, and concentration of flavor, although it is also considered a light, fruity wine. Both have a grapeyness and are berry flavored and jammy. They are often best if served a bit chilled and are good paired with light, simple summer fare. A great picnic wine.

WHITE WINES

WHITE BURGUNDY: Made from chardonnay grapes. These are oaky and buttery, with hints of lemon, spice, and flowers. There's a great range in style among white burgundies, from fuller, heavier bodied to lighter wines. They go well with fish dishes, especially salmon, and cream sauces, as well as light pastas and various kinds of lightly prepared meats, such as veal.

WHITE BORDEAUX: Made primarily from the sauvignon blanc grape. It is lighter, crisper, more acidic. Often described as herbaceous, grassy, appley, and lemony. Goes best with lighter, simpler foods.

A subcategory of white Bordeaux is **SAUTERNE**, which is a dessert wine made primarily from the semillon grape. It is sweet, honeyed and syrupy, and is excellent with desserts, especially fresh fruit or custards.

LOIRE: Made from the chenin blanc or sauvignon blanc grape. They are light, crisp, acidic wines, known for their flintiness or smokiness, as well as grassy or herbaceous characters. These benefit from being served a little colder and are drunk fairly young, usually three to four years from the date on the bottle. They tend to go well with seafood, especially oysters, clams, crabs, and scallops and other light fish or salad dishes. Also great with vegetable soup.

ALSATIAN: This is a huge category of wine, but the two most famous types are made from the riesling grape and the gewurztraminer grape. These wines are much like the German-style white—steely, highly acidic, and crisp, with a spiciness and fruitiness. These wines go well with Chinese food and Indian food, as well as pork, quiche, or German cuisine.

Note: Many mistake "fruitiness" to mean sweetness, particularly in Alsatian and German wines. Typically, in fact, these wines are very dry on the tongue, with very little sugar.

CHAMPAGNE

This is the sparkling wine made in the Champagne region of France, from a mix of grapes—predominantly chardonnay and pinot noir. There are two types, vintage and nonvintage. Vintage means that the wine was made predominantly from grapes of a particularly excellent year. While vintage champagnes are more expensive, the difference in quality between a vintage and nonvintage (a blend of grapes and wines from different years to conform to a house style) is small, so average drinkers gain little from the extra cost of vintage champagne. Champagne varies from light, crisp, and acidy to heavy, toasty, and yeasty. Try different brands of champagne to learn which is to your liking.

Champagne goes with just about everything, except perhaps Mexican and other very spicy foods. Like other wines, champagne is also best served not too cold. And even though the loud pop associated with opening a champagne bottle is a festive tradition, the quieter the better. The louder the sound, the more gasses and bubbles escape, ruining champagne's wonderful effervescent quality. Slip the cork out as gently and as slowly as possible.

ITALIAN WINES

RED WINES

BAROLO: Made from the nebbiolo grape. It is full, warm, robust; has a slightly greater alcohol content than its very close relative, Barbaresco. This wine must be aged for a minimum of three years before it is bottled. It goes with full-bodied, spicy foods, such as tomato sauces, lasagna, roasted meats, and pizza.

BARBARESCO: Also made from the nebbiolo grape. It has many of the same qualities as Barolo but is a bit lighter, not as tannic, and fruitier. Aged for a minimum of two years, it goes with the same foods as Barolo.

CHIANTI: The best known of Italian red wines, it is a simple red wine, not very tannic and lighter bodied. The predominant grape variety is sangiovese. It is best with basic Italian foods such as pizza.

VALPOLICELLA: A relatively light and fruity wine, it nevertheless has some substance. Age improves this wine only up to a point; it should be drunk five to eight years after the date on the bottle. The more basic corvina and molinara grapes are its ingredients. It goes well with simple Italian foods.

WHITE WINES

In general, Italian whites are crisp, light, fruity, and not very woody. They tend to be clean and acidy, almost lemony. Their flavors stand up well to vinaigrettes and seafood dishes.

PINOT GRIGIO: A fine, full-bodied wine that ranges in color from pale straw to copper. This is a very simple wine made from the pinot gris grape. It complements deep-fried seafood dishes and other simple foods.

ORVIETO: Made from the trebbiano grape, this is a medium-bodied dry wine. It goes well with seafood.

FRASCATI: Also made from the trebbiano grape, with the malvasia. A medium-bodied, dry wine, it goes well with lighter Italian foods, particularly seafood.

SOAVE: A crisp, fruity wine made from the garganega and trebbiano grapes. Light and simple, it goes well with the same light fare.

WORLDWIDE VARIETIES OF WINES

In the United States, the most popular wines are from California, which in some cases now equals and even surpasses France in the quality of wine produced. Many other states, particularly in the Northwest, also produce surprisingly good wines. Other countries of the world, like Australia, New Zealand, Chile, Argentina, and South Africa, are also gaining renown for producing high quality wines at cheap prices.

RED WINES

CABERNET SAUVIGNON: This is made from the same grape as the primary grape in French red Bordeaux and is similarly cassis-, cherry-, sometimes eucalyptus-, woody-, and cedar-like. It, like the red Bordeaux, pairs well with roasted meat (including fowl) dishes and other meals with medium to strong flavors.

PINOT NOIR: This is the American version of a red burgundy. Recently, Oregon has gained acclaim in this category of winemaking.

CALIFORNIA DISASTER

California produces about 90% of all wine manufactured in the U.S. In the Earthquake of 1906 in San Francisco, thirty million gallons of wine were lost. The most notable loss was at the Italian Swiss Colony Winery, where the largest wine tank in the world cracked during the quake, spilling half a million gallons of wine over the surrounding area.

MERLOT: Similar in flavor but with less tannin than Cabernet Sauvignon, this wine has more obvious fruit flavors (especially plum) and is less astringent. For this reason, winemakers often blend the two types to round out the flavor of Cabernet Sauvignon.

MALBEC: With plum and anise as its most distinctive flavors, malbec is less prevalent in stores today because of the fragile nature of the malbec grape to extreme weather conditions. Malbec wines from Argentina tend to age better than those from France.

SHIRAZ (or **SYRAH**): Made from the syrah grape, the high tannin content of these wines makes them mature slowly. When young, the flavor of a Shiraz is dominated by strong spice and pepper flavors, but at maturity the taste of blackberries, black currants, plum, and a hint of smokiness come to the forefront. Australia is known for high-quality Shiraz wine.

ZINFANDEL: This wine is indigenous to America but similar to the Rhone wines of France—big, full-bodied, peppery, and heavy. It goes well with heavy foods, such as barbecue, chili, and garlicky foods.

WHITE WINES

CHARDONNAY-BASED WINES: Made from the same grape used to produce French white Burgundy. One of the most popular wines in America, it has a unique complexity and clarity. This wine emphasizes the more

---

TANNIN

Tannins are a chemical compound found in grape skins, stems, and seeds (and also in some of the wood used in wine barrels). They have a strong influence on wine flavor that changes as the wine ages. Since both tannins and coloration come largely from the grape skin, red wines usually contain more tannins than white wines.

If a high-tannin wines (like many of the Italian reds as well as reds made from Syrah and Cabernet Sauvignon grapes) are drunk while young, the tannins cause the wine to dry out the mouth and form an unpleasant coating on the teeth. However, when these wines are properly aged, the tannins soften the taste and add greatly to its complexity. Low-tannin wines are meant to be drunk right away, as aging will not improve their flavor.

If you find yourself suffering with a glass of young, high-tannin wine, eating a high-fat cheese between sips will keep the tannins from coating your teeth.

oaky and fruity aspects, while these qualities of the French version are more balanced by acidity. It complements the same foods as its French counterpart.

SAUVIGNON BLANC-BASED WINES: Made from the same grapes used in French Bordeaux wine. There's more acid and fruitiness and less wood in these wines than in the French white Bordeaux, but they complement the same foods.

SPARKLING WINES

Made in the champagne style, sparkling wines cannot legally call themselves champagne. Nonetheless, these wines can be quite excellent—much a match for their French counterparts. The same serving guidelines apply.

OTHERS

WHITE ZINFANDEL: This wine is still very popular. It is light, crisp, and easy to drink, and goes well with any light fare.

ROSÉ: A light pink wine made from red grapes. The skins are removed before fermentation begins, so only some of their color remains in the wine. Rosé is light, crisp, and not necessarily sweet.

BLUSH: A mixture of white and red wine, with white the predominant ingredient. The wine has all the characteristics of the white used as its base.

FORTIFIED WINES

Fortified wine contains brandy or other spirits, added in order to increase alcohol content or to stop the fermentation process.

These wines are typically sweet, although some are dry. The drier ones are sometimes used as dessert wines or after-dinner drinks. More and more, fortified wines can be found not only on their own but mixed in cocktails, such as the Madeira Cocktail, the Prince of Wales, the Tuxedo, The Affinity Cocktail, the Adonis, the Soviet Cocktail, and the Sherry Twist. Madeira, marsala, port, and sherry fall into the fortified wine category.

MADEIRA

Named for the island on which it is produced, these wines are fortified with brandy made from Madeira wine. They can range in taste from light and dry to heavy and sweet. The types are:

SERCIAL ("rainwater"): light, dry

VERDELHO: light, dry; rare

BUAL: golden, sweet

MALMSEY: deep gold, very sweet

> STARTING OFF RIGHT
>
> In 1801, Thomas Jefferson spent 12% of his yearly salary on wine. His favorite types were Bordeaux and Madeira.

MARSALA

Developed in the 1800s, these wines come from Marsala on Sicily. The wines are warm golden yellow in hue and have a caramel aroma. For the most part they are used for cooking. The important types are:

FINE: must have at least 17% alcohol and be aged for a minimum of four months

SUPERIORE: sweet and dry; must have at least 18% alcohol and be aged for a minimum of 2 years

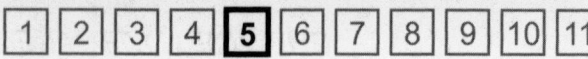

VERGINE: extremely dry; must have at least 18% alcohol and be aged for a minimum of 5 years

SPECIALE: made with eggs and other flavorings; must have at least 18% alcohol and be aged for at least six months

PORT

Originally from Portugal and now associated with England, most ports are red; all are sweet. The types are:

VINTAGE: bottled two years in wood after the vintage and aged for decades; this is a fortified wine of the most excellent quality

RUBY: young and fruity; bright in color

TAWNY: paler, less sweet, and softer than ruby port

WHITE: made from white grapes; similar in taste to ruby

SHERRY

Authentic sherry is made in Spain; sherry-like wines are made, however, in a variety of places, including Australia, Cyprus, and California. The types, ranging from pale and dry to deeply rich and sweet, are:

OLOROSO: golden, full-bodied, can be dry but is usually sweet; cream sherry is the most common variety; sweeter olorosos should be served at room temperature, drier ones on the rocks.

MANZANILLA: very pale and dry; serve chilled

FINO: pale and dry; serve chilled

AMONTILLADO: pale gold and not as dry as fino; fuller in body; serve at room temperature straight or on the rocks

SELECTING & HANDLING THE PROPER GLASS

Wine glasses come in many styles, and each has distinctive characteristics. The proper shape of a wine glass depends on its placement of the wine on the tongue and the extent to which it releases the wine's aroma.

Basically, white wines (especially those that are more mature and fuller-bodied) tend to go in the more stereotypical wine glass shape, that with a large body and straight opening. The large bowl allows the aroma of the wine to reach the nose, while the straight sides help direct the wine to the sides and back of the tongue first, so that the acidity and complexity of the wine flavor can be noted before the sweetness (tasted when the wine hits the tip of the tongue). Younger white wines, with sweetness as their primary feature, tend to work best in glasses with smaller bodies and enlarged openings so that the wine hits the tip of the tongue first.

Rosé wines are primarily sipped from glasses with much shorter bowls than those used for white wines, but with just as large a circumference so that the aromas are released and directed to the nose properly. The size of the opening, as with white wines, depends on the age and sweetness of the wine.

Red wines, if young, are served from glasses similar to those used for mature white wines. More mature and fuller-bodied wines, however, should be served from glasses with both taller and wider bodies (sometimes referred to as a "balloon glass") so that the wines can receive maximal oxygenation and therefore release the most complex aromas towards the opening. This opening is narrower than the body so that the aromas become concentrated and routed towards the nose. The straight sides along the opening make sure that the wine is first delivered to the back of the mouth, Here, the tongue is most able to recognize the robust flavors characteristic of these wines while avoiding contact with the gums, which do not respond well to the astringency of the tannins if they come into contact with one another immediately when the wine enters the mouth.

THE TOASTMASTER GLASS

In the 18th century England, there was a special glass made especially for the Toastmaster of an event. These glasses had a thick bottom and very thick bowls so that they appeared full when only holding a small amount of liquid. This was to help the Toastmaster with his arduous task of remaining standing through all toasts, finishing his entire glass after each was completed.

The glasses used for fortified wines tend to be much smaller than those used for the other types, since these wines are rich and are therefore served in much lower volumes. These glasses have relatively tall bodies for their size that taper towards the top and then grow into larger openings. The height helps the complex aromas develop while the opening directs the wine to the tip of the tongue so that the sweetness balances the other strong flavors.

Regardless of the shape, your glass should always be held by the stem so that your hand does not heat the wine (especially important when drinking white wines), and so that fingerprints on the glass remain at a minimum.

WINE TASTING

Fingerprints are more than a nuisance for whoever gets stuck washing the dishes; they can alter your perception of the first part of the wine tasting experience: the appearance of the wine. The color and clarity of the wine should be observed for each wine. Secondly, the smell of the wine should be noted as it is released during pouring. The third and fourth parts, as can be expected, are the taste and aftertaste. The taste is considered to be the flavor you experience as the wine first enters your mouth until you

swallow it. The aftertaste is the flavor you taste after swallowing, and the intensity of these flavors varies greatly between wines. There are many subtleties in these last two parts of the wine tasting experience that are only discernible after years of repeated exposure. In other words, the road to wine expertise is paved with practice.

If you're hosting a wine tasting, it is important to only invite the number of people that will comfortably fit in your kitchen, dorm room, or other space in which you'll be holding your tasting. Be sure to think of table space, chairs, and, of course, the number of glasses you have when making your invite list. It's hard to hold a classy affair with Dixie cups and repeated games of Musical Chairs.

If you want to have snack food to accompany the wine and help cleanse the palate, buy only unsalted crackers, unflavored bread, or the mildest of cheeses. Any stronger flavors can affect the taste of the wines. Similarly, gum, mints, or even cigarette smoke can alter taste as well, so ask your guests to avoid them. For those who violate your request, have them drink plenty of water before they begin sampling the wines. Also be sure to have plenty of water available for guests to rinse their mouths between wines. You'll also need to provide a container

"BREATHE"

When wine is exposed to the air, it "ages" and mellows. Breathing can thus enhance the flavor of any wine that is too astringent. Simply removing the cork from the bottle and letting it stand will accomplish nothing, since only a very small portion of wine is exposed to air. Pour the wine into a glass or decanter, allowing it to mix with the air, and let it stand for a minute or two. The exposure will soften the flavor.

into which your guests can spit their rinse water. To avoid disaster, this container should be easily distinguishable from a wine glass.

When attending a wine tasting, make sure you keep any negative opinions to yourself. This is especially important when the tasting is held at the vineyard in which the wines were produced. It is also customary, at a vineyard tasting, to purchase at least one bottle of wine. It is perfectly acceptable to ask for a second tasting of a few wines to help you decide which one you'll be taking home. In this respect, wine tasting can be much easier than dating.

RESTAURANT SURVIVAL

Getting a date can be hard enough. Now, you're also expected to pair a wine with dinner. Don't worry, as the waiter or sommelier (a member of the restaurant staff whose sole purpose is to help customers select wine) will be there for you. As party size increases, it becomes harder to select one bottle that will accompany each dinner well. In these cases, it is best to order either multiple bottles of wine or wines by the glass. Whichever route you choose, don't be afraid to ask questions.

If you are new to the world of wine or just don't want to risk making a fool of yourself, feel free to leave your wine choice mostly up to the waiter. He or she will probably present several options that vary in price, so you'll most likely find a wine in your price range. If you have a question about a wine and aren't sure how to pronounce its name, it isn't uncommon or unacceptable to point to the description and let the waiter say it for you. Some people like to avoid this game by referring to the wine by

the bin number if it is listed alongside the name of the wine. If you're fairly experienced with wine pairing, feel free to make your questions to the waiter more specific, like "I'd like a Cabernet Sauvignon to accompany my rack of lamb. Which would you recommend?"

If you order a bottle of wine for the table, make sure you know the preferences of each wine drinker. If your table is split between red and white wine fans, choose a wine of either color that is closer to the middle range, such as an oaky Chardonnay or the low-tannin Pinot Noir. This is just to ensure that the waiter has indeed brought the correct bottle and just requires a simple nod before the waiter uncorks the bottle. While some still believe that the host should smell the cork to make sure the wine isn't tainted in any way, this practice is considered to be unnecessary and rude in most restaurants today. The waiter will almost undoubtedly know if the cork indicates any problem with the wine.

After uncorking the bottle, the waiter will pour a small amount in the glass of the host. If this is you, watch while the waiter pours the wine to observer its appearance, then pick up and hold the glass under your nose while swirling the wine inside to release the aroma. Next, taste the wine and, after swallowing, ob-

HISTORY OF TOASTING

The word "toast" came from the Roman tradition of placing a piece of toasted bread into a communal wine glass to improve the flavor. The person who drank the last of the wine claimed the toasted bread from the bottom of the cup. The tradition of touching glasses came in the 17th century, when the sound of clinking glass was thought to repel the devil.

serve the aftertaste. Unless the wine is clearly spoiled or tainted in some way, nod or say something to the waiter that affirms that this wine is in fact the wine you ordered. It is not acceptable to send back a bottle of wine just because you don't like the taste or it isn't what you expected.

The waiter will then begin filling the glasses of those drinking the wine at your table, ending with the host. When all of the glasses are full, you may either make a toast or unceremoniously begin to drink the wine. Enjoy!

STORING WINE

In storage, keep wine bottles on their sides so the corks will stay moist, and protect them from temperature and light. As a general rule, serve red wine at room temperature and white wine chilled. "Room temperature" generally refers to that which is found in Europe (and especially England). Americans consider 72 degrees to be room temperature, while the English consider 50 degrees to be somewhere near the norm. Consequently, a red wine served at 50 degrees will generally taste sprightlier than the same wine served at 72 degrees. So, putting a *little* chill on a red wine definitely makes it more palatable.

CHAPTER 6:
INNOVATIONS
WITH BEER, WINE,
& CHAMPAGNE

Too often dismissed, the delights of wines, beers, and champagnes can expand into numerous other areas. Which is not to say that an aromatic glass of red wine or a frosty mug of beer are not satisfactory in their own right; quite the contrary, it is with good reason that the bartender spends most of her time filling glasses with these drinking staples. Still, a number of creative approaches to these alcohols allow for some bold innovations that highlight just how profound and powerful they can be. This chapter attempts to do some justice to beers, wines, and champagnes (in order) by exploring the mixed drinks that they can produce.

BEER DRINKS

Are you the kind of connoisseur whose favorite cocktail is a beer straight from the can? You'll be amazed at what you can do with your old standby – and we're not just talking about shotgunning it. Serve the following drinks in a beer mug or pilsner glass. If you are serving from a keg of beer and have no idea how to use the pressure tap, see Chapter 8.

Black Velvet

1 part porter or stout
1 part champagne (extra dry)

Pour these carefully down the side of the glass to make two distinct layers. In all, 10 to 16 oz.

Half-and-Half

1 part ale
1 part porter or stout

In all, 10 to 16 oz.

Shandy Gaff

1 part beer
1 part ginger ale

In all, 10 to 16 oz.

Boilermaker

1 shot whiskey
1 mug full of beer

Add a jigger of whiskey to a mug of beer. You can (a) drink the whiskey and chase it with the beer (boring), (b) pour the shot into the beer (better), or (c) drop the shot – glass and all – into the mug of beer and chug it all down quickly before it foams all over you. This is sometimes called a "depth charge." Beer and whiskey, mighty risky!

Hop-Skip-and-Go-Naked

1 oz. vodka
1 oz. gin
juice of ½ lime
beer to fill

Serve over ice. To serve as a punch, measure the ingredients by the bottle and case while using 12 limes.

Beer Buster

1½ oz. vodka
beer to fill
2 dashes of Tabasco sauce

Stir lightly in a mug or pilsner glass.

Snakebite

1 part beer
1 part cider

In all, 10 to 16 oz. This drink is a favorite of jolly olde Ireland, and its mildly sweet flavor attests to the lack of vicious serpents in the said land.

Root Down

1 shot root beer schnapps
3/4 glass of beer

Fill a beer glass three-quarters full with beer, then drop in the shot of schnapps (for the gamut of possible techniques, refer to the Boil-ermaker). In one single and dramatic quaffing gesture, down the entire concoction, which should taste just like root beer. The shot glass, however, does not taste like root beer – do not swallow glass!

WINE DRINKS

Kir

dash crème de cassis
dry white wine, chilled, to fill

Served in a wine glass.

Spritzer

1 part white wine
1 part club soda
garnish with a lemon twist

Served on ice in a large wineglass or tall, frosted highball glass.

Vermouth Aperitif

Serve sweet vermouth on ice with a lemon twist.

150

Vermouth Cocktail

1 oz. sweet vermouth
1 oz. dry vermouth
soda water (after shaking the vermouths)
dash Angostura or orange bitters
garnish with a cherry

Add ice to the sweet and dry vermouths, stir, and strain into a wineglass. Fill with soda water.

CHAMPAGNE DRINKS

Arise My Love

½ oz. green crème de menthe
champagne

Served in a champagne glass.

Caribbean Champagne

splash rum
spash crème de banane
champagne to fill
garnish with a banana slice

Served in a champagne glass.

Champagne Cocktail

glass of champagne
2 dashes bitters
1 tsp. sugar
garnish with an extra-long spiral twist of lemon peel

Stir without ice.

VERMOUTH

Vermouth is an aperitif, named from the Latin "aperio" meaning "to open," in recognition of the fact that vermouth is supposed to excite the appetite and whet the palate before meals. The beverage is made from a neutral, dry white basic wine which is then infused with herbs and aromatic delights. While its Latin roots would seem to encourage a bottle of vermouth to be opened, one needs to take care to avoid skunking the beverage. The herbs dissipate once the bottle is opened unless it is re-capped and refrigerated. Aged vermouth that is left to breathe outside a refrigerator will quickly become stale, losing its residency in the kingdom of Flavor Country.

Diamond Fuzz

1½ oz. gin
1 oz. sour mix
1 tsp. sugar
champagne to fill (after shaking all other contents)

Shake gin, sour mix, and sugar. Strain into a highball glass with ice, and then fill with champagne.

French 75

1 oz. gin
1 oz. sour mix
2 tsp. sugar
champagne to fill (after shaking all other contents)
garnish with an orange slice and a cherry

Shake gin, sour mix, and sugar with ice. Strain over fresh ice into a highball or Collins glass. Then add champagne to fill.

Kir Royale

dash crème de cassis
chilled champagne to fill

Serve in a champagne glass.

Mimosa

1 part champagne
1 part orange juice
dash triple sec (optional)
garnish with an orange slice

Midori Mimosa

2 oz. Midori
2 tsp. lime juice
champagne to fill
garnish with a lime wedge and strawberries (optional)

COOLERS

Serve these drinks over ice in tall, frosty glasses. At a busy bar, if a customer orders a wine cooler or spritzer, just pour about 3 oz. of wine over ice in a tall glass and fill with soda water. Since most coolers are made with wine or champagne, we've dumped the liqueur-based coolers into this section as well.

Champagne Cooler

1 oz. brandy
1 oz. Cointreau or triple sec
champagne to fill
garnish with mint sprigs

Country Club Cooler

3 oz. dry vermouth
1 tsp. grenadine
soda water to fill
garnish with an extra-long lemon spiral

Pineapple Wine Cooler

2½ oz. dry white wine
2½ oz. pineapple juice
½ tsp. powdered sugar
1 oz. rum (optional)
soda water to fill
garnish with a lemon and an orange twist (extra-long spirals)

Red Wine Cooler

3 oz. red wine
7-Up, Sprite, or soda water to fill

White Wine Cooler

3 oz. white wine
7-Up, Sprite, or soda water to fill

Apricot Cooler

1½ oz. apricot brandy
club soda or ginger ale to fill

Boston Cooler

2 oz. rum
2 oz. club soda
½ tsp. sugar
club soda or ginger ale to fill
garnish with lemon twist (extra-long spiral) and an orange slice

Stir 2 oz. of club soda and sugar in a highball glass. Add rum and cracked ice, then fill with club soda or ginger ale. This is a fizzier version of the Rum Collins.

Gin Cooler

2 oz. gin
2 oz. club soda
½ tsp. sugar
club soda or ginger ale to fill
garnish with lemon twist (extra-long spiral)
    and an orange slice

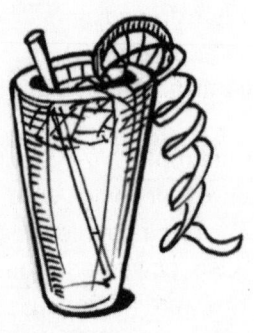

Stir 2 oz. of club soda and sugar in a high-ball glass. Add gin and cracked ice, then fill with club soda or ginger ale.

Rum Cooler

2 oz. light rum
2 oz. club soda
½ tsp. sugar
soda water or ginger ale to fill
garnish with lemon twist (extra-long spiral) and an orange slice

Stir 2 oz. of club soda and sugar in a highball glass. Add rum and cracked ice, then fill with club soda or ginger ale.

Scotch Cooler

2 oz Scotch
splash crème de menthe
soda water to fill
garnish with mint sprigs

Tequooler or Tequila Cooler

1½ oz. tequila
juice of ½ lemon or lime
tonic water or soda water to fill
garnish with a lemon twist (extra-long spirals)

Vodka Cooler

2 oz. vodka
2 oz. club soda
½ tsp. sugar
club soda or ginger ale to fill
garnish with lemon twist (extra-long spiral) and an orange slice

Stir 2 oz. of club soda and sugar in highball glass. Add vodka and cracked ice, then fill with club soda or ginger ale.

CHAPTER 7:
NOVELTY DRINKS, PUNCHES,
& NON-ALCOHOLIC DRINKS

Rarely ordered in a bar, novelty drinks provide an intriguing and unusual change of pace. Both for their multifarious palate and the aesthetic displays that often accompany them, novelty drinks can add an illusion (or the actuality) of refinement to your drink-making lexicon. Most of the beverages in this chapter prove delightful for special events, whether for private parties that you're hosting or for a quick recovery from seasonal chills. This chapter is divided into four categories: hot drinks, for picturesque moments of languid, wintry bliss; flaming drinks, for the dramatic bartender; punch recipes, for both conventional and unconventional means of serving the masses at a tasteful fête; and light and non-alcoholic drinks, because people who aren't getting liquored up deserve to enter Flavor Country, too.

HOT DRINKS

There's nothing like a piping hot drink on a cold day, a truth that gains even more validity when you add some booze for extra warmth. While not nearly as popular as the mixed drinks of the previous chapter, all of these potent concoctions can still get you completely snokkered with cheer. Most of these drinks specify an ingredient or two to be added to a non-alcoholic hot drink such as coffee, cider, or tea. For mixing purposes, assume that the serving size of that drink is what you would drink normally – about 5 to 8 oz. The drinks are listed alphabetically for easy reference.

COFFEE DRINKS

Bailey's Coffee
1½ oz. Bailey's Irish Cream
hot black coffee
whipped cream on top after stirring

Caffé di Amaretto
1½ oz. amaretto
hot black coffee
whipped cream on top after stirring

Café Mexicano
1 oz. Kahlúa
½ oz. tequila
hot black coffee
garnish as desired after stirring

Irish Coffee
1½ oz. Irish whiskey
1 tsp. sugar
hot black coffee
whipped cream on top after stirring

Jamaican Coffee
1 oz. Tia Maria (or Kahlúa)
¾ oz. rum
hot black coffee
whipped cream on top after stirring (optional)
dust of nutmeg on top

Kahlúa Irish Coffee

1 oz. Kahlúa
1 oz. Irish whiskey or Bailey's Irish Cream
hot black coffee
garnish as desired after stirring

Kioki Coffee

1 oz. Kahlúa
½ oz. brandy
hot black coffee
garnish as desired after stirring

Mexican Coffee

1½ oz. Kahlúa
hot black coffee
whipped cream on top after stirring (optional)
dust of nutmeg or add a cinnamon stick

Tequila can be either substituted for or combined with Kahlúa.

Nutty Coffee

1 oz. amaretto
½ oz. Frangelico
hot black coffee
whipped cream on top after stirring

Nutty Irishman Coffee

1 oz. Irish cream or Irish whiskey
1 oz. Frangelico
hot black coffee
whipped cream on top after stirring
sprinkle of chocolate shavings

Roman Coffee

1½ oz. Galliano
hot black coffee
whipped cream on top after stirring

160

OTHER HOT DRINKS

Chimney Fire

1½ oz. amaretto
hot cider
garnish with a cinnamon stick

Chimney Fires can bum ever so brightly in a multitude of colors.
For other flavors, just substitute Southern Comfort or dark rum for
amaretto. To burn your whole house down, drink a lot of these.

Comfort Mocha

1½ oz. Southern Comfort
1 tsp. instant cocoa or hot chocolate
1 tsp. instant coffee
boiling water to fill
whipped cream on top after adding boiling water

Good Night

2 oz. rum
1 tsp. sugar
warm milk
dust of nutmeg

Serve in a mug.

Grog

1½ oz. rum
1 tsp. sugar
juice of ½ lemon
boiling water

Serve in a mug.

Hot Buttered Rum

2 oz. rum
1 tsp. sugar
1 tsp. butter
boiling water
dust of nutmeg

Hot Gold

3 oz. amaretto
6 oz. very warm orange juice
garnish with a cinnamon stick

Hot Toddy

2 oz. whiskey
1 tsp. sugar
boiling water
garnish with a lemon slice
dust of nutmeg or add a cinnamon stick

Serve in a mug.

Hot Wine Lemonade

1½ oz. red wine
juice of ½ -1 lemon
1½ tsp. sugar
boiling water
garnish with a lemon twist

Amaretto Tea

1½ oz. amaretto
1 tsp. sugar (optional)
hot tea
whipped cream on top

Do not stir the amaretto mixture.

Kahlúa and Hot Chocolate

1 oz. Kahlúa
hot chocolate
whipped cream on top

Tom and Jerry

1 egg, separated
2 tsp. sugar
¼ cup hot milk
1 tbsp. butter
1½ oz. rum
½ oz. brandy (float on top at the end)
dust of nutmeg

Heat the milk and butter together until hot. Beat the egg white and egg yolk separately, then add the egg white to the yolk and beat in the sugar. Put the mixture in a warm mug and fill with rum and more hot milk, then stir.

FLAMING DRINKS

Flaming drinks can be a lot of fun when done safely and correctly. They are much less fun if they accidentally result in someone's hair lighting on fire (or worse...). To flame a drink, first warm only one teaspoon of required liquor over a match flame, then ignite. Once it is lit, carefully pour it over the prepared recipe. Stand back! This method is usually safer than lighting the liquor right in the glass.

FLAMING

Nothing says "U!S!A!" quite as dramatically as explosives on the Fourth of July. Sometimes, however, pyrotechnic fervor on this magnificent day takes on different, more inventive dimensions, potentially including the lighting of flaming drinks. If you learn nothing else from this guide, keep this in mind: DON'T FLAME YOUR DRINKS NEAR FIREWORKS. A failure to heed this warning will dramatically increase the likelihood that the bombs won't just be bursting in air. And that's not what the Fourth of July is about.

Café Royale

1 cube of sugar soaked in brandy
1 cup of hot black coffee
cream (float on top at the end)

Ignite sugar in a spoon and drop into the coffee as it caramelizes and the flame dies out.

BLUE BLAZER

Unlike Green Lantern and the Green Hornet, the Blue Blazer is not a superhero. Nevertheless, those who correctly prepare this concoction in the dark (with great care, of course) will become bartending superheroes, as the mixing process is like juggling liquid, blue fire.

Blue Blazer

2½ oz. whiskey
2½ oz. boiling water
1 tbsp. honey (optional)
garnish with a lemon twist

Pour the whiskey and the boiling water into two separate mugs. Ignite the whiskey. Mix by pouring back and forth several times between the two mugs. Serve in a warm rocks glass.

Southern Blazer

1½ oz. Southern Comfort
1 oz. Kahlúa
2½ oz. boiling water
1 tbsp. honey (optional)
garnish with a lemon twist

Pour the alcohol and the boiling water in two separate mugs. Ignite the booze. Mix by pouring back and forth several times between the two mugs. Serve in a warm rocks glass.

Brandy Blazer

2 oz. brandy
1 tsp. sugar
1 piece orange peel
1 lemon twist

Put ingredients in an Old Fashioned or rocks glass. Stir with a bar spoon and strain into a thick, stemmed glass.

Harbor Light

½ oz. Kahlúa
½ oz. tequila
½ oz. 151-proof rum

Layer the ingredients in a shot glass, then ignite.

Lighthouse

2 oz. Galliano
2 oz. dry vermouth
garnish with a lemon slice

Ignite Galliano in a shot glass and pour it over dry vermouth in a cocktail glass. This drink may be served on the rocks in a champagne glass.

PUNCHES

So you're a little shy about pouring in public? Try some of these punch recipes so that you can show off your new bartending abilities while still mixing in the comfort and privacy of your own home. All of the following recipes should be served from a punch bowl with a large block of ice in it, unless directions specify otherwise. For each serving, ladle about 4 oz. into a plastic lowball glass.

Brandy Punch

juice of 12 lemons
juice of 4 oranges
sugar
1 cup grenadine
1 cup triple sec
2 liters brandy
2 cups tea (optional)
1 quart soda water
garnish with fruit

Mix the lemon and orange juices, add sugar to taste, then mix with all the other ingredients. Add soda water just before serving. Yields 35 to 50 servings.

Buddha Punch

1 bottle Rhine wine
½ cup curaçao
1 cup rum
1 cup orange juice
1 quart soda water
Angostura bitters to taste
1 bottle chilled champagne
garnish with mint leaves and fruit slices

Add champagne just before serving. One bottle of champagne usually contains 750 mL or one quart. Either size is acceptable. Yields 25 to 30 servings.

Canadian Fruit Punch

2 liters Canadian whiskey
12 oz. can frozen orange juice concentrate
12 oz. can frozen lemonade concentrate
12 oz. can frozen pineapple juice concentrate
1 cup simple syrup (as described in Chapter 1)
3 quarts strong iced tea
garnish with fruit

Yields 65 to 75 servings.

Claret Punch

2 bottles claret (or 1½ liter bottle)
1 cup triple sec
2 cups brandy
sugar to sweeten
juice of 12 lemons
2 quarts soda water

Add soda water just before serving. Yields about 40 servings.

Egg Nog

1 lb. confectioners' sugar
12 eggs, separated
1 pint brandy
1 pint light rum
1¼ quart milk
1 pint heavy cream
sprinkle of nutmeg on top

Beat confectioners' sugar in with egg yolks. Stir in slowly: brandy, rum, milk, and cream. Chill. Fold in stiffly beaten egg whites before serving – don't beat or stir the whites. Do not serve with ice. Yields 45 to 65 servings.

Fish House Punch

juice of 12 lemons
powdered sugar
1 liter rum
1 bottle brandy (750 mL)
½ cup peach brandy
2-3 quarts cola, flavored soda, or lemonade
garnish with citrus fruits

Be sure to add enough sugar to sweeten the lemons. Yields 25 to 35 servings.

French Cream Punch

1 cup amaretto
1 cup Kahlúa or coffee brandy
¼ cup triple sec
½ gallon softened vanilla ice cream

No ice. Mix well. Yields 15 to 20 servings.

Fruit Punch

1 liter vodka
1 bottle white wine
2 12 oz. cans frozen fruit juice concentrate (pineapple, grapefruit, or orange)
2 quarts soda water

Add soda water just before serving. Yields about 40 servings.

Gin Punch

2 liters gin
1 pint lemon juice
2 cups cranberry juice cocktail
1 quart orange juice
½ cup grenadine
1 quart soda water
garnish with sprigs of mint

Add soda water just before serving. Yields about 45 servings.

Green Machine

2 liters vodka
1 12 oz. can frozen limeade concentrate
½ pint lemon sherbert
½ pint lime sherbert

Yields about 35 servings.

Hot Apple Rum Punch

1 liter dark rum
1 quart apple cider
2 or 3 cinnamon sticks, broken
1½ tbsp. butter

Heat in saucepan until almost boiling. Serve hot. Yields about 15 servings.

Hot Mulled Wine

3 cups water
2 cinnamon sticks, whole
8 cloves
peel of 1 lemon, cut into twists or into one long spiral
1 cup sugar
1 bottle dry red wine
splash brandy (per glass while serving)
garnish with lemon slice (per glass)

Boil everything except the wine in a large saucepan for 10 minutes, then add the wine. Heat but do not allow to boil. Just before serving add a splash of brandy and a lemon slice to each glass. Serve hot. Yields 15 to 25 servings.

Oogie Pringle Punch

1 liter rum
1 quart pineapple juice
1 quart cranberry juice
garnish with lemon slices

Yields about 25 servings.

Party Punch

2 cups sugar
1 cup water
2 cups concentrated fruit syrup
2 cups orange juice
2 cups pineapple juice
2 bottles chilled champagne
2 quarts ginger ale
1 quart soda water

Boil the sugar and water for five minutes, then add all the fruity goodness (syrup and juices). Just before serving, add the champagne, ginger ale, and soda water.

Planter's Punch

1 liter rum
1 pint Jamaican rum (Myers's)
1 pint fresh lime juice
1 pint simple syrup (as described in Chapter 1)
1 quart soda water
garnish with orange slices and cherries

Add soda water just before serving. Yields about 30 servings.

Planter's Punch (Variation)

1 liter rum
1 cup Jamaican rum (Myers's)
1 cup curaçao (optional)
1 pint lemon juice
1 cup orange juice
1 cup pineapple juice
garnish with orange slices and cherries

Yields about 20 servings.

170

Red Wine Punch

2 bottles dry red wine
1 pint lemon juice
1 cup simple syrup (for recipe, see Chapter 1)
1 cup raspberry syrup
2 quarts soda water

Add soda water just before serving. Yields about 40 servings.

Rum Fruit Punch

1½ liters rum
½ pineapple, sliced
1 pint strawberries
¾ cup simple syrup (for recipe, see Chapter 1)
1 cup lemon juice
2 cups pineapple juice
1 pint thinly sliced strawberries
2 quarts soda water

Chill everything except the strawberries and soda water for two hours. Just before serving, add the strawberries and soda water.

Sangría

2 bottles rosé wine
3 oz. curaçao
2 oz. brandy
1 cup orange juice
½ cup lemon juice
¼ cup sugar
1 liter club soda
30 oz. can fruit cocktail
3 sliced oranges
garnish amply with fruit

Just before serving, add the soda water.
Yields 35 to 40 servings.

Sangría Maria

1½ liters hearty burgundy wine
1 quart ginger ale
4 oranges sliced into wedges
2 lemons sliced into wedges
2 peaches sliced into wedges
any other fruits you wish to add
garnish with lemon slices, orange slices, and cherries

Let stand for at least two hours. Strain into punch bowl with ice.
Yields about 25 servings.

Narri's Sangría

2 cups dark rum
1 quart sweet red wine
1 quart dry red wine

This recipe comes from the bar of Narri, a former manager of the
Harvard Bartending Course. Soak cut-up fruits (strawberries, or-
anges, lemons, limes, and whatever you like) overnight in the rum.
Then add the wines before serving. Yields 25 to 30 servings.

Southern Comfort Punch

1 bottle Southern Comfort (750 mL)
2 cups grapefruit juice
1 cup lemon juice
2 quarts 7-Up, Sprite, or ginger ale

Yields about 30 servings.

Sparkling Pink Punch

1 bottle rosé wine
1 bottle chilled champagne
1 10 oz. container thawed whole frozen raspberries or strawberries

Pour champagne and wine over the fruit. Yields about 15 servings.

Supersonic Nog

1 liter Kahlúa
1 liter vodka
4 quarts prepared dairy egg nog
dust of nutmeg or cinnamon

Yields about 40 servings.

Tequila Punch

1 liter tequila
3 liters sauterne
2 quarts fruit cubes and balls (8 cups)
1 bottle chilled champagne

Sweeten to taste. Add champagne just before serving. Yields about 45 servings.

Tropical Punch

5 bottles white wine
1 lb. brown sugar
1 quart orange juice
1 pint lemon juice
5 sliced bananas
1 pineapple, cut or chopped
3 liters light rum
1 pint dark rum
2 cups crème de banane
garnish with fruits

Blend the wine, sugar, juices, and rums. Cover and let stand overnight. Add the rums and crème de banane before straining into a punch bowl over ice. Yields about 100 servings.

Velvet Hammer Punch

1 bottle sauterne
12 oz. apricot brandy
1 liter vodka
1 bottle chilled champagne
1 quart ginger ale

Add champagne and ginger ale just before serving. Yields about 30 servings.

Wedding Punch

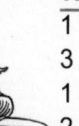

1 liter vodka
3 cups orange juice
1 cup lemon juice
2 quarts ginger ale
garnish with cherries, lemons, and orange slices

Yields about 35 servings.

Welder's Punch

1 liter vodka
1 quart ginger ale, 7-Up, or Sprite
1 quart fruit punch
1 quart orange juice
garnish with orange slices and cherries

Yields about 35 servings.

Whiskey Punch

2 liters bourbon
½ cup curaçao
1 quart apple juice
juice of 6 lemons
2 oz. grenadine
4 quarts ginger ale
garnish with cherries

Add ginger ale just before serving. Yields 60 to 65 servings.

174

Wine Punch

1½ lbs. sugar

2 quarts soda water

2 bottles dry red wine

1 pint brandy

1 pint rum

1 bottle sparkling white wine

garnish with sliced oranges and pineapple slices

Dissolve the sugar in the soda water before adding the red wine, brandy, and rum. Before serving, adding the sparkling white wine. Yields 45 to 50 servings.

CHAMPAGNE PUNCHES

Champagne Punch

2 or 3 bottles chilled champagne

½ cup curaçao

½ cup lemon juice

1 quart soda water

½ lb. confectioners' sugar

Mix this punch just before serving. Yields 25 to 35 servings.

Champagne Punch (Variation)

½ cup brandy

½ cup Cointreau or triple sec

2 bottles chilled champagne

Yields about 15 servings.

Champagne Punch (Variation)

½ cup light rum
½ cup dark rum
juice of 2 lemons
juice of 2 oranges
1 cup pineapple juice
½ cup sugar
2 bottles chilled champagne

Add champagne just before serving. Yields about 20 servings.

Champagne Punch (Variation)

6 oranges
sugar
4 bottles champagne
1 bottle Mosel wine

Slice and arrange oranges on the bottom of a punch bowl. Sprinkle with sugar and add wine. Just before serving, place an ice block in the bowl and add chilled champagne. Yields about 30 servings.

Champagne Holiday Punch

1 bottle chilled champagne
2 quarts ginger ale
1 can crushed pineapple with juice (8 oz.)
1 quart raspberry sherbert

Mix this punch just before serving. Yields 25 to 35 servings.

Champagne Rum Punch

2 liters rum
1 bottle sweet vermouth (750 mL)
1 quart orange juice
1 bottle chilled champagne
garnish with sliced bananas

Add champagne just before serving. Yields about 40 servings.

176

Champagne Sherbert Punch

1 quart lemon or pineapple sherbert
2 bottles chilled champagne
1 bottle sauterne
garnish with lemon slices and/or pineapple chunks

Put sherbert in first. Yields about 25 servings.

NON-ALCOHOLIC PUNCHES

Cardinal Punch

2 quarts cranberry juice
1 quart orange juice
juice of 4 lemons
8 bottles of ginger ale

Add ginger ale just before serving over ice.

Fruit Juice Combo

1 cup tomato juice
1 cup V-8 (or other vegetable juice)
1 cup apple juice
1 cup cranberry juice
1 cup grapefruit juice
1 cup lemonade
1 cup orange juice
1 cup pineapple juice
8 drops Tabasco sauce
garnish with a skewer of fresh pineapple, orange, and apple slices

Skewer is used to stir. Serve over ice in a highball glass. Makes 8 servings.

Fruit Punch

36 oz. water
1 12 oz. can frozen grape juice concentrate
1 12 oz. can frozen lemonade concentrate
1 12 oz. can frozen orange juice concentrate
1 quart ginger ale
1 pint raspberry sherbert

Mix the water and concentrate. Add
ginger ale before serving, then
spoon the sherbert over the punch.

Kentucky Derby

1½ cups sugar
2 cups cold water
1 cup lemon juice
2 quarts ginger ale
garnish with lemon slices and mint sprigs

Long Island Tall Boy

6 oz. can lemonade concentrate
1 quart orange juice
garnish with strawberries and lime slices

Makes 4 to 8 servings.

Red Rooster Punch

4 cups V-8 (or other vegetable juice)
10 oz. ginger ale
1 tbsp. lime juice
1 tsp. Worcestershire sauce
dash Tabasco sauce

Makes about 6 servings.

Snoopy Punch

1 12 oz. can frozen lemonade concentrate
1 12 oz. can frozen fruit punch concentrate
1 pint pineapple sherbert
3 lemons, sliced
1 quart ginger ale

Add ginger ale just before serving. If you serve this punch to anyone over 12, you may want to give it a different name. Something tough, like No Limit Gangsta Punch.

Strawberry Punch

1 pint fresh strawberries
1 13½ oz. can sweetened, condensed milk

Blend with ice and serve in lowball glasses.

Sunset

3 cups V-8 (or other vegetable juice)
½ tsp. horseradish
½ tsp. Worcestershire sauce

Makes 4 servings.

Unreal Champagne

1 cup sugar
2 cups water
2 cups grapefruit juice
juice of 1 lemon
2 28-oz. bottles of ginger ale
dash grenadine

Add ginger ale just before serving. Serve in champagne glasses. Makes 15 to 20 servings.

Punch Alternatives

If you aren't thrilled with any of these punch recipes, try converting your favorite highball into punch form. For example, a
Seabreeze contains:

1½ oz. vodka

2 oz. grapefruit juice (approximately)

2 oz. cranberry juice (approximately)

In punch form, this would loosely translate to:

1 liter vodka

2 quarts grapefruit juice

2 quarts cranberry juice

This recipe would make a beautiful, delicious, cool summer punch.
Adapt the ingredients to suit your tastes – add more mixer or vodka
to vary the alcohol content.

LIGHT & NON-ALCOHOLIC DRINKS

Even without alcohol, many of these concoctions are very tasty
and should be an option at any party. As a responsible bartender, a non-alcoholic drink is a necessity that can be used
not only to quench the thirst of non-drinkers, but may also be
an integral tool when deciding to cut someone off. In the past
few years, non-alcoholic beers and wines have become increasingly popular and are a definite plus to have around when
bartending. The selection of these drinks is constantly increasing and gives non-drinkers and designated drivers even more
alternatives to drinking.

The term "light alcohol" in the heading warrants further explanation. Many mixers such as bitters and extracts may contain
alcohol, and great care should be taken in their use. Certain people
may have strong physiological reactions to even the smallest
amounts of alcohol, so a responsible bartender should be aware
of exactly what is going into a "non-alcoholic" drink.

There is an infinite number of combinations of fruit juices that can create potable beverages. Also, many popular drinks can be converted to their "virgin" counterparts simply by eliminating the alcohol in them. Once again, don't be afraid to experiment – you may just invent a popular new drink.

Beach Blanket Bingo

4 oz. cranberry juice
4 oz. grape juice
club soda to fill
garnish with a lime wedge

Serve over ice in a highball glass.

Cranberry Cooler

2 oz. raspberry juice
juice of ½ lime
soda water to fill

Serve over ice in a highball glass.

Fritzer

1 tsp. sugar
2 dashes bitters
soda water to fill
garnish with a lemon twist

Please note that some bitters contain small amounts of alcohol and may be harmful to some non-drinkers.

Grapeberry

4 oz. cranberry juice
4 oz. grapefruit juice
garnish with a lime wedge

Serve in a highball glass over ice.

Innocent Passion

4 oz. passion fruit juice
splash cranberry juice
splash orange juice
juice of ½ lemon
soda water to fill

Serve over ice in a highball glass.

Lime Cola

juice of ½ lime
cola to fill

Serve over ice in a highball glass.

Mickey Mouse

1 scoop vanilla ice cream
cola to fill
whipped cream to top
garnish with two cherries

Topping with whipped cream and two cherries gives the effect of a silly-looking mouse without having to get ripped off in Orlando. Serve with a straw and a long-handled spoon.

Pink Snowman

1 cup orange juice
1 10 oz. package frozen strawberries
2 large scoops vanilla ice cream

Blend and serve with another scoop of ice cream.

Roy Rogers

dash grenadine
cola to fill
garnish with a cherry

Shirley Temple

dash grenadine
7-Up or Sprite to fill
garnish with a cherry

Unfuzzy Navel

4 oz. peach nectar
4 oz. orange juice
juice of ½ lemon dash grenadine
garnish with an orange slice

Shake and serve over fresh ice in a highball glass.

Vanilla Cola

Splash of vanilla extract
cola to fill

Serve over ice in a highball glass. Vanilla extract frequently contains a small amount of alcohol and may be harmful to some non-drinkers.

Virgin Colada

4-6 oz. coconut cream
4-6 oz. pineapple juice
garnish with pineapple chunks and serve in a highball glass

Virgin Mary

tomato juice to ¾ full
small splash lemon juice
dash Worcestershire sauce
dash Tabasco (more for a hotter drink)
shake of salt and pepper
¼ tsp. horseradish (optional)

CHAPTER 8:
THE COCKTAIL PARTY

Cocktail parties are like relationships – they can be extremely satisfying, an utter nightmare, or somewhere in between. Unlike relationships, however, the right combination of people isn't always enough to guarantee a good cocktail party. While it's true that a roomful of rotten human beings will usually make for a bad time in any situation, even a party full of your closest friends could turn sour if you fail to plan properly.

Good cocktail party planning involves four steps: buying the right supplies, setting it up, keeping the bar supplied as the party progresses, and knowing when and how to throw everyone out. If you follow each step properly, things should go smoothly. At the very least, if you've planned a good party, you can feel free to blame anything that goes wrong on bad luck. Or bad guests.

Guests are actually the single most important factor in planning and running a party. At almost every step, what you need to do varies according to the kind of party you're having – and the kind of guests you're inviting. For example, if you're having 30 nuns over for drinks, you'll want to buy very different supplies than if you invited the same number of marines. By the same token, if you're

planning a 20-keg fraternity party, you'll want to set up the bar (or bars) differently than you would for Uncle Phil's retirement party, (Obviously, this depends on what kind of person your Uncle Phil is. But you get the point.) Just keep in mind that you're trying to maximize your guests' enjoyment and adjust accordingly.

STEP 1: GETTING THE RIGHT SUPPLIES

This is probably the most important step in putting together a successful party. Your guests will forgive you if you put the vodka in the wrong place on the bar or forget to refill the peanut dish, but if you run out of liquor 45 minutes into a three-hour party, you're not going to make anyone very happy. Although the exact items you may need vary considerably depending on the party, there are certain basic items – liquor, beer, mixers, ice, etc. – that you will need to have on hand for any occasion. Once again, keep your guests in mind as you decide what you'll need.

First, you have to decide what kinds of drinks you would like to serve. The basic cocktail bar includes the following:

At least two kinds of light alcohol: gin and vodka (usually rum as well and sometimes tequila – especially if any Texans will be in attendance).
At least two kinds of dark alcohol: Scotch and bourbon (usually also blended whiskey).
Two vermouths: dry and sweet.
Wine: white and red (probably also rosé and fortified wines like port or sherry).
Beer
A selection of non-alcoholic drinks.

Five variables will influence your liquor decisions:

SEASON: In warm weather, people tend to order light alcohols, beer, and white wine. Conversely, in winter, stock up on dark alcohols, coffee drinks (such as Irish coffee and Mexican coffee), sherry, brandy, and red wine.

AGE: Younger people usually prefer light alcohol, blended drinks, wine, beer, and sweet-tasting liqueur cocktails. Older guests drink more dark alcohols, usually unmixed. Buy the highest quality, most prestigious brands you can afford for older, whiskey-drinking guests. They will recognize and expect better names.

HOLIDAYS, THEMES & SPECIAL OCCASIONS: If the party theme or a holiday season lends itself to special drinks, alter your bar's offerings accordingly. Serve egg nog, hot mulled wine, or punch at a Christmas party; champagne on New Year's Eve; mint julep on Kentucky Derby Day; green-colored beer on St. Patrick's Day; a red or pink "love potion" punch on Valentine's Day. If your boss is indicted for embezzling funds and has to flee to Mexico, serve margaritas at his going-away party. He probably won't be attending, but he would no doubt appreciate the gesture.

TIME OF DAY: At 10 a.m. brunch bar, don't expect to be making many Zombies, or even gin and tonics. Instead, concentrate on mimosas, screwdrivers, and Bloody Marys. Before dinner, serve light aperitifs – drinks to stimulate appetites, not anesthetize them: for instance, wine, like cocktails, Dubonnet, and Kir. As a general rule, add more liquor and more variety as the day progresses, culminating with a fully stocked bar for the 8 p.m. to 2 a.m. crowd.

GUESTS' PREFERENCES: Use your own judgment for other bar adjustments. If your best friend drinks only Sombreros, keep a bottle of Kahlúa at the bar.

LIQUOR

For a typical four-hour cocktail party, buy one liter of hard alcohol for six guests. Feel free to adjust according to the drinking habits of your guests. Make sure you buy the one-liter size because it's easier to handle; larger bottles may cost less per drink, but they are bulky, heavy, and often won't take speedpourers. Also, unless you're giving an informal party at home, think twice about buying large bottles and pouring the liquor into smaller containers – this "marrying" of bottles is illegal in many states. Also, you will need only one bottle of each vermouth.

Give a reasonable amount of thought to brand-name selection. Two factors should govern which brands you buy: your budget and your desire to impress the guests. If you're financially secure and you're coordinating a party for the boss – buy premium liquor (the name brands considered the highest quality, and usually the most expensive). On a more limited budget for a party with the neighbors – or your current in-laws – you can get by with call brands (good quality, recognizable brands, but usually cheaper than top shelf). For a fraternity party – or a party for your ex-in-laws – buy bottom-shelf or generic liquor. Remember that most students have very few qualms about drinking "Funky Town" vodka. If you're making punch, you can usually get away with using cheaper brands as long as you mix the punch well out of sight of your guests.

If you must economize, buy cheaper brands of light alcohols: they usually go into mixed drinks, so guests can't taste brand differences. Cutting corners here will allow you to spend more on the higher quality dark alcohols, which people often drink unmixed. For a more extensive discussion of liquor quality and brand selection, see Chapter 1.

To save money without sacrificing name-brand prestige, consider mixing weaker drinks. Make 1¼ oz. or a 1 oz. highball and the liquor bottles won't empty as quickly. Be careful, however – this may make your harder-drinking guests irate.

When you order for a large party, ask in advance at your local liquor store if you can buy on consignment, a deal that allows you to return any unopened, sealed bottles for a refund after the party. Some stores charge extra for this service but in some situations it's worth the cost.

BEER

For standard, four-hour cocktail parties, plan on about one case of beer (24 beers) for every 10 guests. Keep in mind that younger crowds tend to drink much more beer than older ones, and the quality of beers differs even more widely than that of liquors. If you're having 35 guests or more, consider purchasing a quarter keg (about 7.8 gallons – the equivalent of more than three cases, or 83 12 oz. servings). For 70 guests, buy a keg (technically a half keg, which contains 151½ gallons – about seven cases, or 165 12 oz. servings). Keg beer is economical in the long run, but you will have to leave a deposit on the keg and tap. For the best-tasting beer, move the keg to its party location at least four hours before the party and keep it consistently cold until empty. Put it in a big tub or barrel, pack chunks of ice around it (try for block ice, which won't melt as fast as cubed or cocktail ice), and cover it with a big plastic bag or towel.

Most kegs use a standard pressure-tap. Take hold of the two small outcropping handles attached to the ring at the base and turn counterclockwise. Then place the tap on the outlet and turn the ring clockwise to screw it into the keg. If you did not turn the ring far enough in the clockwise direction, you may find yourself soaked in beer. You can raise the pressure on the stream of beer flowing out by pumping the tap; you can lower the pressure by pulling on the small release pin at the base of the tap. The first few beers coming out of the keg will usually be very foamy. You will have to pump the tap periodically to keep a steady stream flowing as the level of beer in the keg decreases. A very small minority of taps works differently from this one; don't hesitate to ask for more information at the liquor store when you pick up the keg.

WINE

The amount and kind of wine you'll need varies from party to party. The heavy wine-drinking group (not to be confused with "winos" – a classification that connotes addling about in public while knocking back a paper bag full o' cheap wine) may consume three or more glasses per person whereas an older crowd gathered during cold weather would drink only half a glass per person. One case (12 bottles) of wine contains about 60 servings. Generally speaking, younger crowds drink more than older crowds, although they also tend to be less picky – you might just be able to get away with that four-liter jug of red (something that you shouldn't attempt with a more sophisticated crowd). White wine is more popular in warmer weather, whereas fortified wines, reds, brandies, and sherry are more appropriate in the winter. Ask for help at your liquor store or look for a slightly dry inexpensive white wine.

Wine comes in bottles containing 750 mL, 1½ liters, and 3 liters, and occasionally even larger bottles. Buy whatever size costs the least. It is perfectly appropriate to transfer wine from large bottles to carafes for serving ease and attractiveness.

PUNCHES

For any gathering of 15 people or more, it might be easier to serve punch in addition to or even instead of other drinks. Punches are especially appropriate for the holiday season, and serving a punch will cut down considerably on the amount of time spent in mixing drinks. Moreover, a good punch recipe will amaze and impress your friends with very little effort on your part. (See the punch recipes in Chapter 7.) The amount you need depends on the strength of the punch; count on about four or five servings per person.

MIXERS

For every liter of light liquor that you have, you'll need about two quarts of mixers. The most common light-alcohol mixers are tonic water, fruit juice, and cola. Whiskey drinkers tend to add less to their liquor, so you can get away with buying less of dark-alcohol mixers such as soda water, ginger ale, and light soft drinks (1 to 1½ quarts per liter). Estimate how much of each mixer you'll need and then buy a few extra liters of fruit juice and soft drinks in order to accommodate non-drinking guests. Also, make sure you have diet soda on hand if you're expecting weight-conscious guests.

ICE

Believe it or not, ice is probably the most important of all cocktail ingredients. If you run out of blended whiskey or gin, guests can at least switch to something else. There are no substitutes for ice, however, and just about anyone who's ever had a rum and Coke at room temperature will tell you that it's unpleasant. For a typical four-hour party, plan on 1 lb. of ice per person. In winter, you could get away with only ¾ lbs., and in summer you should buy 1½ lbs. per guest. If you want to fill an ice chest for beer and wine, remember to get enough to fill the chest in addition to cocktail ice needs. Check the Yellow Pages or ask at your liquor store; you may be able to find a local company from which you can order ice in quantity (by the 40 lb. bag, for example). Some places will deliver right to your home on the day of the party. Make sure to specify cocktail ice when you order so that you don't end up taking an ice pick to a 40 lb. bag (or, in frustration, any of your guests).

GARNISHES

For a basic bar, limes and lemons are essential, while orange slices are optional. Buy one lime for every four to six guests and cut the limes into wedges in advance. Cut lemons into twists and slices and cut oranges into slices; you'll need a supply of lemons and oranges to the tune of about one per 25 guests. Consider buying a jar of olives (a must for Martinis), cocktail onions (optional – only if you're inviting a Gibson drinker), and cherries (for Manhattans). Fruit-cutting instructions and additional suggestions abound in Chapter 2.

FOOD

You shouldn't consider having a cocktail party of any size without offering some sort of food along with the drinks. At the very least, buy some peanuts, chips, or other snacks. Appetizers – cold vegetables and dip, cheese and crackers, or even more complicated hors d'oeuvres – are better. For more information, buy a cookbook.

UTENSILS

The basic bartending kit described in Chapter 2 – available from Harvard Student Agencies – should take care of your utensil needs. Also make sure that you have at least one trash barrel, a large ice bucket, a sharp knife for cutting fruit, a water pitcher, a towel, and an ashtray for the bar. An ashtray may seem like a minor detail at this point, but if a line forms at the bar, any smokers in the group will invariably end up flicking burning embers wherever gravity takes them (a disaster if they land in the punch!).

NAPKINS

Remember to put out some cocktail napkins for your guests. For a nice touch, place the stack of napkins on the bar, put a shot glass in the center, and bear down firmly as you twist the glass clockwise. Remove the glass and you've created an attractive fanned design of cocktail napkins. Oh-la-la!

GLASSWARE

Real glassware adds a touch of class to any party; on the other hand, broken glassware doesn't. You may want to opt for disposable plastic glasses, which are perfectly acceptable for even relatively high-brow gatherings. You need only two types: the lowball or on-the-rocks, which is short and wide and holds about 9 oz. and the highball, which is taller and holds 10 to 12 oz. Use the highball for popular highballs, beers, Collinses, and the lowball for everything else – stirred cocktails, shaken drinks, on-the-rocks liquor and wine. For a four-hour party, at least three per person, at a ratio of 75% highball to 25% lowball. For a dance party, plan on at least four per person; people tend to put the glasses down when they feel the Night Fever and then forget about them.

If you insist on real glasses, check the phone book for a general rental agency. Some will even deliver glasses to your home and pick them up again after the party.

STEP 2: SETTING UP

Once you've gathered all your supplies together, you'll need to set them up in as efficient and attractive a manner as possible. The bar itself can be nothing more complicated than a table that's strong enough to support the weight of all the bottles and the occasional sideways lurch by a tipsy guest. Cover it with a plastic tablecloth for protection from spills and with a linen tablecloth over that if you're aiming for a classy appearance.

For small parties (fewer than 15 people), you don't need a bartender. A self-service bar, set up like the one in Diagram 1, provides room for two guests to mix their own drinks. Parties of 20 to 100 people tend to run more smoothly with the help of a bartender. Diagrams 2 and 3 illustrate two possible setups for a one-person bar.

Large parties of over 100 guests require the services of at least two bartenders. In Diagram 4, notice that the two bartenders share the mixers but have their own liquor bottles for speed and efficiency's sake.

Are you already tired of all this planning? Can't afford a big bash? Have a BYOB party instead – bring your own bottle. At a BYOB, each guest brings a contribution to the bar. It's impossible to diagram a BYOB setup (or outcome), so you'll just have to improvise.

Use common sense in setting up the party room. Avoid locating it near a doorway, where it will invariably block traffic. Try to put the bar against a wall; if you're tending bar yourself, set it up so that guests can't sneak around you and pour their own drinks. If this happens, your carefully planned, efficient layout will deteriorate rapidly, and in time your bar will be a mess. To avoid this fate, make an example of any people who try to cross into the bartender's territory by saying to them, "I would appreciate it if you stepped back."

STEP 3: WORKING THE PARTY

Once the party actually starts, your primary – and perhaps only – concern should be the maintenance of a smoothly running bar, making sure that it remains orderly and well stocked. The ease with which these tasks can be accomplished depends on the type of party you're having, but as long as you succeed in this challenge, all should be tickety-boo.

Diagram 1: Self-Service Bar

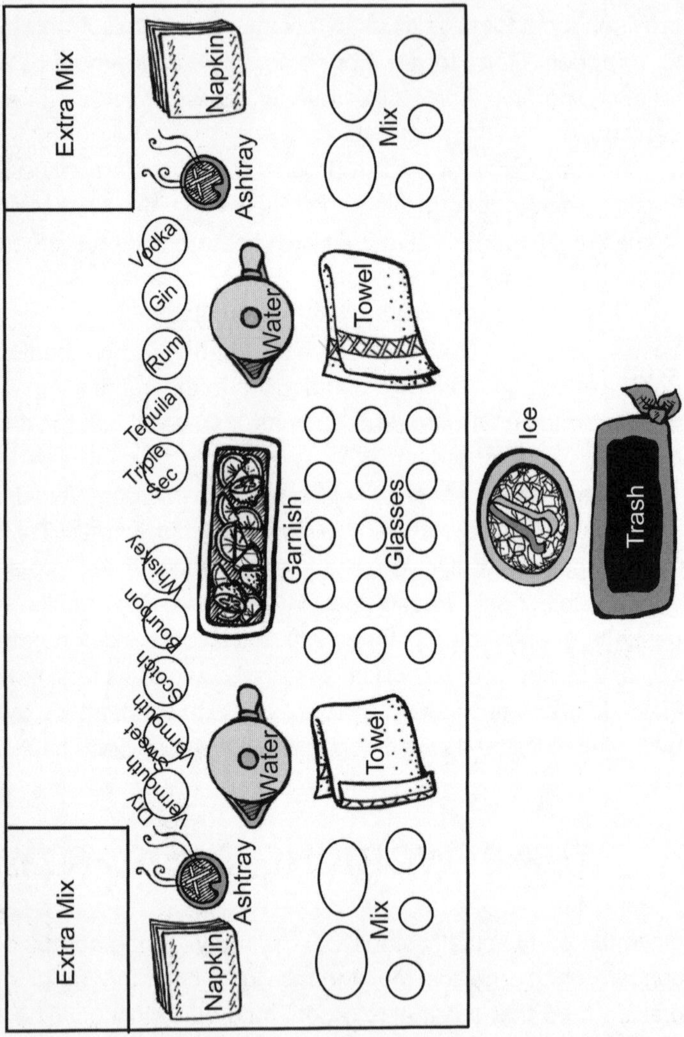

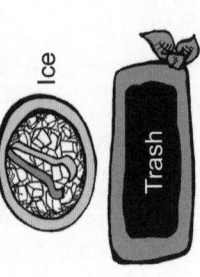

Extra Mix

Napkin

Ashtray

Vodka
Gin
Rum
Tequila
Triple Sec
Whiskey
Bourbon
Scotch
Sweet Vermouth
Dry Vermouth

Water

Towel

Mix

Garnish

Glasses

Ice

Trash

Extra Mix

Napkin

Ashtray

Water

Towel

Mix

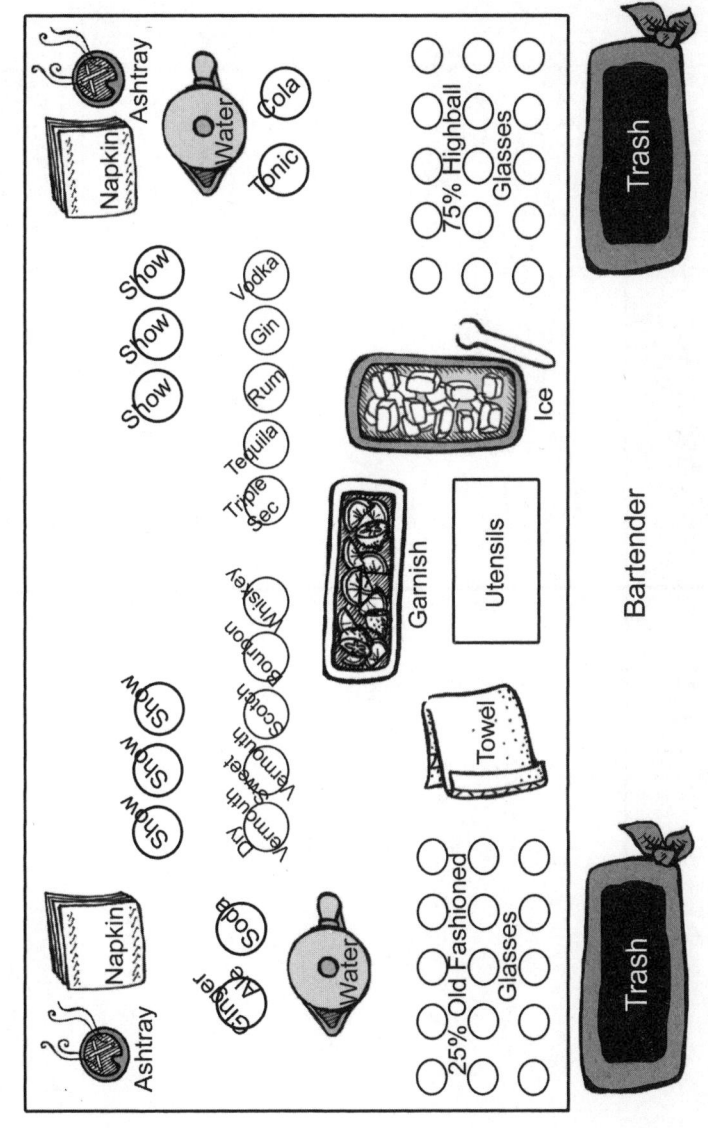

Diagram 2: One-Person Bar

198

1 2 3 4 5 6 7 **8** 9 10 11

Diagram 3: One-Person Bar

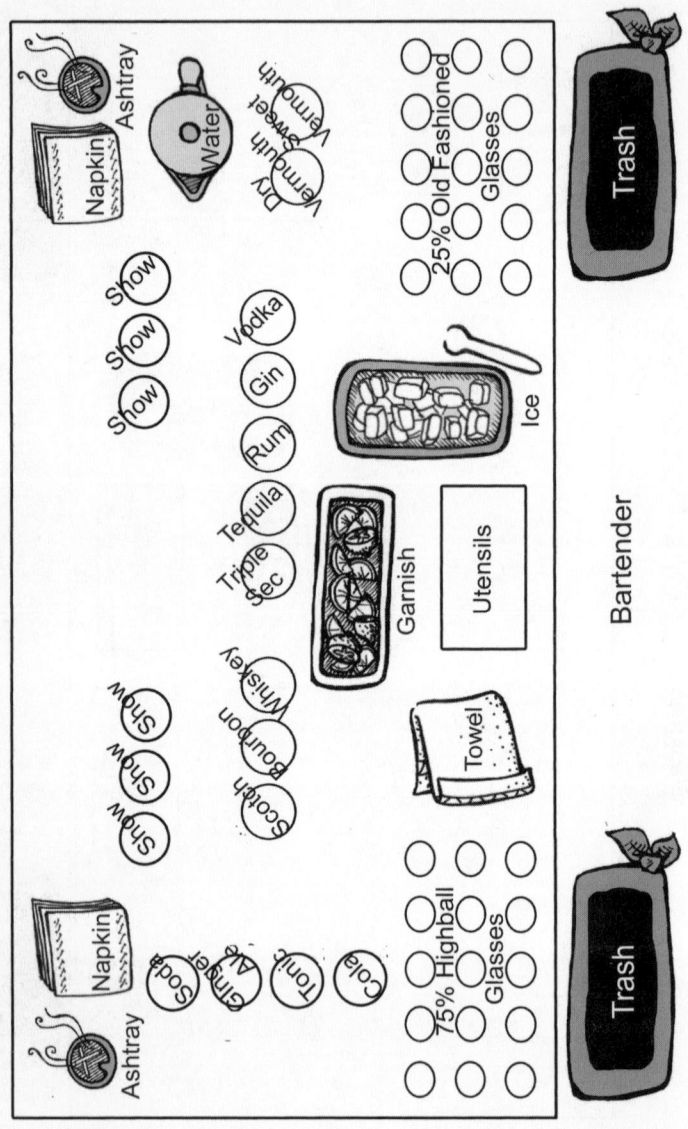

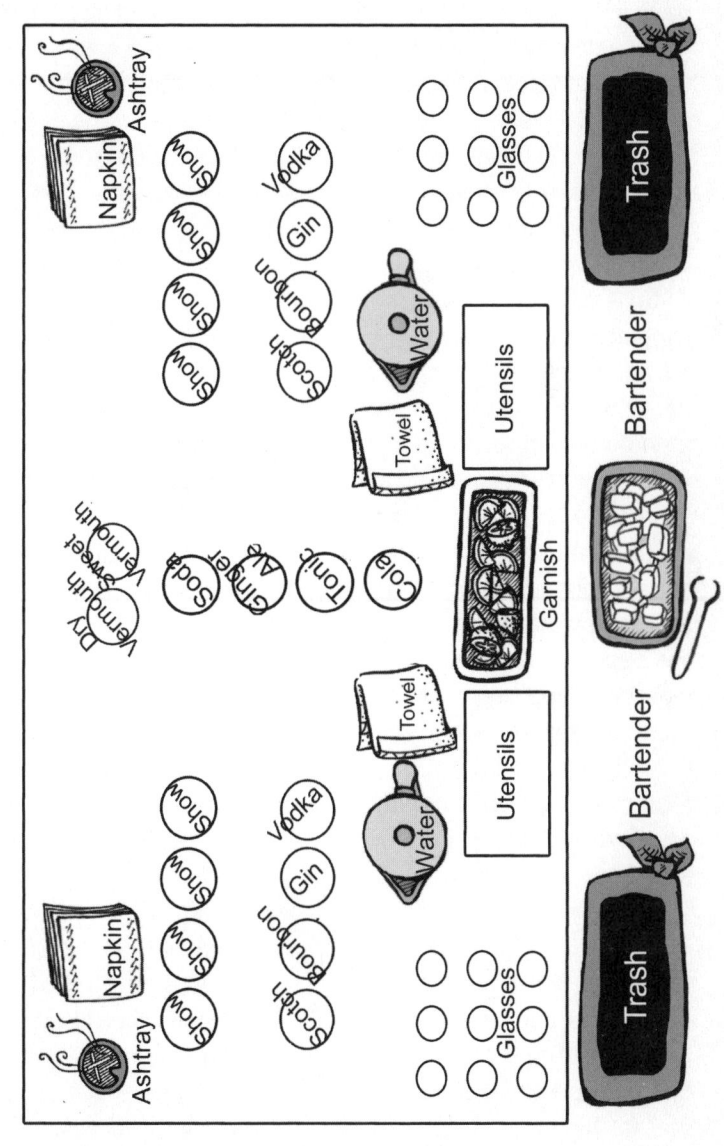

Diagram 4: Two-Person Bar

Unless guests are mixing their own drinks, keeping the bar orderly should be simple – just put all of the bottles and utensils back in their original place after you use them and you shouldn't have to do much more than pick up the occasional empty glass or wadded-up napkin. Take advantage of lulls in the action – whenever the bar clears out for a minute, take the time to tidy things up.

Keeping things supplied is a little more challenging. You'll invariably need to replace items like ice and mixers that may be as far away as the kitchen. This is complicated by a fundamental rule of bartending – never leave the bar unattended – and its corollary – if you leave it unattended, all hell will break lose and people will be jumping out the windows by the time you return. The rule holds true for nearly any gathering; even otherwise respectable, trustworthy adults will occasionally show the restraint of hyperactive, foaming-at-the-mouth children when left alone around a fully stocked bar.

So you've run out of ice and you're trapped behind the bar. What to do? Simply ask a friend, a co-worker, or anyone else who's available and won't mind helping to get another bag of ice. If you're in a situation where you don't know anyone at the party, look around for wallflowers (the folks who spend more time hovering around the peanut dish than talking to other guests). Every party has at least one, and he or she will probably welcome the sudden moment of attention before returning to the ignominy of loneliness.

It's a good idea to keep a snack – nothing more complicated than peanuts or pretzels is necessary – somewhere near the bar so guests who are waiting for drinks will have something with which to occupy themselves.

For more details on how to look and act professional behind the bar, read Chapter 9. One professional prerequisite discussed there calls for some clarification here: tips. At a private party, a tip cup on the bar looks extremely tacky. On the other hand, if you work at an "impersonal" party, such as a large company gathering or some sort of dance, guests may appreciate the option of bribing you for faster or stronger drinks. In situations like this, ask the person who hired you if you may put out a tip cup. If you use one, put a dollar in at the beginning of the night to give guests a hint.

STEP 4: THROWING EVERYBODY OUT

This is actually much easier than it sounds. When you're ready to call it a night, simply start putting the bar away. First, pack up extra liquor and mixers and take them to the kitchen. Then take speedpourers out of the remaining bottles, put the caps on, and put those bottles away. Guests will quickly notice the absence of liquor; some will be annoyed, but most will eventually start heading home.

At this point, keep a careful eye out for guests who have had too much to drink. Never let an intoxicated guest drive home. This is not only extremely dangerous, but also legally actionable – party hosts can be sued for damages caused by drunken guests. If you find yourself in such a situation, either ask a sober guest to drive them home or call a cab.

ORDERING SUMMARY

Liquor: 1 liter per 6 guests plus beer and wine
Mixer: 2 quarts per liter of light alcohol
  1 quart per liter of dark alcohol
  a selection for non-alcoholic drinks
Ice: ¾ lbs. per person in winter
  1 lb. per person in moderate weather
  1½ lbs. per person in summer
  more as needed to fill wine and beer chests
Garnishes: 1 lime per 6 people (more in summer and for young
    people)
  1 lemon per 25 people
  1 orange per 25 people (optional)
Glasses: 3 per person (more for a dance party)
  75% highball
  25% lowball
Snacks: vary widely

PARTY CHECKLIST

Use this checklist –and your own common sense – as a guide when planning your party. Don't feel obligated to buy everything listed (unless your pockets are very deep); as always, tailor your purchases to the needs of your guests.

Liquor
bourbon
blended whiskey
Scotch
vodka
gin
rum
tequila
beer
wine
dry vermouth
sweet vermouth
other liquors?

Equipment
shaker glass and shell
jigger
speedpourers
bar spoon
ice bucket
corkscrew/bottle
opener/can opener
ashtrays
bar napkins
water pitcher
dry and wet trash buckets
swizzle sticks/cocktail straws

Garbage/Garnishes
lemon twists and slices
lime wedges
orange slices
olives (pitted and without pimentos)
specialty garnishes (optional)
maraschino cherries (with stems)
cocktail onions

Mixers
tonic water
cola
soda water
ginger ale
Sprite or 7-Up
diet soda
sour mix
Bloody Mary mix
mixing juices
light cream
milk
water
Rose's Lime Juice

Glassware (Plastic)
lowball
highball
beer
wine

Condiments
bitters
bar sugar
nutmeg
grenadine
salt
Tabasco sauce
horseradish
Worcestershire
pepper
(You might consider purchasing a pre-fabbed Bloody Mix at the liquor store in lieu of many of these ingredients.)

CHAPTER 9:
PROFESSIONAL
BARTENDING

This is it – you've patiently learned every trick of the trade. You can set up a bar, throw a good cocktail party, mix any one of a hundred drinks in the blink of an eye, and even converse intelligently about the genealogy of gin. And now, you want what every good American wants: a paycheck.

And why not? Whether you're looking for part-time work or a full-fledged career, bartending can be both a fun and an interesting job. Furthermore, you can make a pretty good living at it in some of the choicer bars. In the first half of this chapter, we'll tell you how to find a job – where and how to look for a place that fits your talents. In the second half, we'll tell you how to act on the job – what to wear, what to do, and what not to do as a professional bartender.

LOOKING FOR A JOB

High employee turnover makes bartending an ideal job to break into. If you hit the right place at the right time, presto – well… okay, it's not quite that easy. Remember how we explained each drink-mixing process as though a two-year-old child could get it? When you start dealing with professional bars, it's not quite that simple. Working in a high-class bar requires speed and efficiency, and the only way you can develop these skills is through experience. No matter how many times you carefully read Chapter 2 or how many drink recipes you diligently memorized in Chapter 3, you will not be able to stroll into the Ritz tomorrow and land a job. Chances are, you'll have to start near the bottom of the proverbial totem pole before working your way up.

The good news here is that the bottom of the bartending world isn't necessarily the worst place in the world. You don't have to start out in a miserable spot where the boss is an ape and the customers are baboons. Rather, "bottom" generally refers to places where you won't make much money – the low salaries, poor customers, and empty bar rooms won't pay your rent. Compensation for hard work at the bottom comes in the form of the speed, efficiency, and experience that you will gain so that you can move up to the next, higher-paying tier.

There are a number of different types of businesses that hire bartenders. They are listed below in roughly ascending order according to the amount of experience you need to get hired. Keep in mind, however, that this will vary considerably according to the individual business. Extremely posh catering services, for example, will probably be more selective than those that cater to Little League banquets. Of course, most Little League banquets won't require a bartender anyway... unless it's an event from one of those nefarious national teams that fudges the ages of its players.

1. Catering or Temporary Services
Bartending at catered events is usually an undemanding experience, and most caterers are willing to hire people with little or no experience. Unfortunately, tips (if allowed) are not very large at catered events, and you probably won't make a lot of money at these jobs. The best way to find a caterer in your area is to check the Yellow Pages.

2. Hotel with Banquet Facilities
These are very similar to catering jobs; most are low pressure and low paying. Frequently, hotels will have an office for hiring staff of all varieties, making it the right place to inquire about available jobs.

3. Harbor Cruises

This option is obviously limited to people who live near large bodies of water. Also known as "booze cruises," these jobs are usually a little more demanding than catering work (not least because some people find the combination of seasickness and liquor to be unsettling). Most of the companies that offer these cruises have offices directly on the docks. Tips will vary depending upon who rents the boat.

4. Airport/Train State Bars

These are also low-pressure jobs. Unfortunately, tips are usually terrible. Many times these bars are owned by outside corporations that pay rent to the airport/station in exchange for space, so a manager might be harder to track down in person. Be persistent; jobs in these venues are easier to come by than you might think.

5. Hotel and Restaurant Bars

These vary widely depending on the quality of the hotel or restaurant. In larger restaurants, you can find work at the service bar, where you'll make drinks to be served by the waiters and waitresses. These provide good experience, but since you won't be in contact with the customers, you will frequently not get tips (although some establishments will include service bartenders in the pooled tips collection).

6. Local Bars without Large Crowds

These are your typical neighborhood bars: cozy, friendly, and usually quiet (think about what *Cheers* looked like most of the time). If there's a strong contingent of "regulars" (Norm and Cliff excepted), you can make decent tips. However, the less crowded the bar, the fewer tips you'll get.

7. Public Bars

These are the large-capacity, crowded bars and nightclubs where customers stand two or three deep at the bar on the weekends and the bartenders are usually run ragged until closing time. These are the highest-paying jobs, but they're also the most demanding. Don't expect to land one of these jobs without experience.

Perhaps you are asking yourself, "How do I get a job at one of these here places?" One of the first things you'll have to do is to stop talking to yourself – bars don't like to hire folks whom they perceive as crazy. There's no single method that guarantees success; however, there are a few different approaches that you can take.

APPLY DIRECTLY TO THE MANAGER

Find a place that looks appealing, stroll right in, and ask to see the manager. If they're not currently hiring, they might be soon; leave a résumé or make sure that the manager knows how to contact you if an opening emerges. Never look for work during peak hours, since both the manager and the rest of the employees will probably be busy preparing and will resent you for interrupting them. The best time to approach a bar looking for work is between 2 and 4 p.m., when the manager should be around while not overwhelmed with work. Never ask another bartender if that particular place is hiring; they will almost always say no, regardless of the truth of the matter, since bartenders often have other bartending friends (presumably not you) whom they would like to see hired.

USE PERSONAL CONNECTIONS

As in any job hunt, personal connections should not be underestimated. If you happen to be the friend of a bartender, you've got a leg up on anyone else who is applying. An acquaintance with a current employee who can provide you with a good recommendation is a definite advantage.

BE WILLING NOT TO START AS A BARTENDER

There are essentially two bar jobs other than bartending – working the door and working as a barback. If you're hired by a bar and you don't have much experience, chances are you'll be asked to start at one of these jobs and work your way up to tending bar in a couple of months. Beware of bait-and-switch tactics on the part of the manager – if it becomes clear that he or she has no intention of promoting you, it might be a good idea to start looking for another job.

Working the door is essentially a dead-end job. You'll be able to pick up a fair amount of knowledge about how a bar is run, but you won't get any hands-on experience. Working as a barhand, on other hand, is a much better way to learn the bartending trade. A barback, also known as "bar rat" in seedy and less-flattering environs, is essentially a bartending apprentice. Your responsibilities would include tapping kegs, running ice, replacing glassware, stocking garnishes, and so on. You'll have the opportunity to observe closely the bartenders whom you're backing up, so keep your eyes open, file away any questions that come to mind, and query the bartenders whenever there's a lull. If you develop a good relationship with your bartenders (in the professional sense, of course), you may be asked to set up drinks (that is, put everything in the drink except the alcohol). After a few weeks of this type of experience, you should be ready to make the move to bartending.

OFFER TO TAKE A SLOW SHIFT

You may not have a choice in this matter. Slow shifts such as lunch bar shifts, Sunday brunches, and possibly Monday or Tuesday nights offer the same pluses and minuses as working in an uncrowded bar; you'll be under less pressure to perform although your tips won't be as substantial.

DON'T LIE ABOUT YOUR EXPERIENCE

Outright lying about or merely exaggerating your experience might get you a job, but it's a poor idea. Bartending is a learned craft, and if you lie your way into a job that's beyond your experience level, you'll be found out after an hour and quite possibly thrown out on your rear. Lying is so wrong and [somewhat dated presidential joke deleted – eds.].

LOOK FOR SEASONAL WORK

Summer and winter tourist spots usually hire many more employees during the high season. The advantages are obvious – not only are there more job opportunities and more customers (meaning bigger tips), but you'll also probably be working near either a beach or a ski slope. If you want to find this sort of summer work, start looking far in advance. For example, if you want a summer job on Cape Cod, start your search when there's still snow on the ground and all the other would-be bartenders are still skiing. Cruise ships also offer interesting bartending opportunities as long as you're prepared for a major lifestyle change. Most hire out of Miami and New York.

FIND OUT IF A LOCAL UNION HAS A REFERRAL SERVICE

In some cities, the local Hotel and Restaurant, Institutional Employees, and Bartenders Union offers a job referral service to its members. Large hotels, restaurant chains, and other unionized establishments sometimes hire directly through the union, so mem-

bership will spare you the tedious door-knocking that might otherwise be necessary. Call your local union to inquire; if it doesn't have a referral service, don't bother to join – there's no point in paying union dues when you're unemployed.

CULTIVATE CURRENT EMPLOYERS AS REFERENCES

Never consciously alienate an employer, regardless of his or her ogre-like leanings. When you're looking for that prestigious second (or third or fourth) job, your potential future employer will want to know how well you performed in your previous position. Be prepared to provide names and phone numbers of former employers as references. If you really did annoy your last boss, it's probably not a good idea to list him or her as a reference.

DON'T GET DISCOURAGED

Finding a first job can be tedious and frustrating. Above all, don't get discouraged. Be persistent and patient. Speak as politely in your 40th interview as you did in your first. Emphasize how hard you'll work and your willingness to accept low pay in exchange for experience.

ACTING LIKE A PROFESSIONAL

APPEARANCE

Bartending is a service profession, which means that only half the job involves making drinks well and efficiently. The other half requires that you make people happy – a bartender has to learn how to please both the customers and the managers at the same time.

A clean, spiffy appearance is crucial for professional bartending. In a restaurant, the manager can hide a grubby, slovenly, vermin-infested cook back in the kitchen if need be. By contrast, bartenders work right up front, handling ice and fruit in full view of the customers. Obviously, a good bartender must look immaculate and well groomed; drinks prepared by a sloppy bartender with dirty hands are rather unappealing.

Most bar managers will tell you what to wear when they hire you; most will request that you wear clothes appropriate to the bar's style. Whatever you wear, always look neat and comfortable so that you can maintain a cool, confident bartending demeanor, even after several hectic hours. If you're allowed to choose your dress in a somewhat fancy place or a catering agency, or if you're self-employed, stick with tradi-  tional bar attire. Men wear dark pants and shoes with a white shirt and a bow tie. The bow tie idea might sound silly, but long ties have an irritating tendency to fall into the drinks that you mix. A bow tie might make you look like Pee Wee Herman (or Tucker Carlson), but it will provide essential freedom of movement. Women should wear a dark skirt or slacks with a white blouse. Long-haired representatives of both sexes should tie their tresses back neatly.

Try to keep your appearance behind the bar as close to neutral as possible. A good bartender is like a good vodka – he or she promotes a pleasant feeling of well-being, but blends easily into many surroundings. Both men and women should avoid wearing flashy jewelry, political buttons, and outrageous clothing; if you have any doubts regarding the neutrality of a hair style or article of clothing, do not sport it. Some bars may promote a hipper, more colorful image, but most prefer the conservative look. Use your own judgment in these matters, but remember that, while your customers probably won't speak up and tell you when your appearance has offended them, they'll pass along a little message in their tips (or lack thereof).

ATTITUDE

In a way, this aspect of bartending is more important than anything else. Mix a screwdriver with the wrong amount of vodka and nobody will notice. Annoy a customer and the whole bar will hear about it.

Whatever happens, look like you know what you're doing. Nine times out of ten, a confident attitude will fool the customer, even if you have no idea what goes in a rum and Coke. If you maintain the image of authority, patrons won't question your ability to mix a drink or your decision to shut off a drunk. Customers and bar managers get uncomfortable when they see their bartender stumbling around and looking noticeably confused, or if they see a scowling, irritable, mumbling bar keep. Always smile (or at least look cocky), grab bottles by the neck surely and swiftly, speak clearly and positively, and act like you know every drink ever invented.

That last word of wisdom needs a bit of clarification. Don't feel mortified if you must ask the customer what goes into a drink. You should feel properly stupid if you don't know how to make a gin and tonic, but nobody expects you to remember what goes into a Pink Squirrel. Don't be afraid to ask, and don't rule out the possibility of bluffing a bit since the customer probably doesn't even know the ingredients of the really exotic drinks. Why embarrass him or her by asking?

If you do completely screw up a drink, you can usually talk your way out of it. One former instructor of the Harvard Bartending Course used to tell the following tale: once, when he was just beginning his illustrious career, a customer ordered a Hop-Skip-and-

Go-Naked. The instructor vaguely remembered that the drink must be pretty strong to merit such a name, so he confidently sauntered to the back bar threw a little of this, a dash of that, a few ounces of flavored brandies, some coloring, several rums, and three garnishes. He presented the piece with a flourish to the customer, who stared at the concoction in horror and protested, "But that's not 1 oz. vodka, 1 oz. gin, and the juice from half a lime, filled with beer!" Without missing a beat, the instructor replied, "Oh! You wanted a Western Hop-Skip-and-Go-Naked! I made you the Eastern version!"

Don't forget that line – you might need it some day. Many drinks vary drastically between regions of the country, bars, or recipe books. Just try to keep on top of the variations as much as possible, and act confident even when you're not.

COURTESY: THE CUSTOMER IS ALWAYS RIGHT (EVEN IF STUPID)

However painful it may be to follow this axiom in practice, the customer is always right. If a patron accuses you of making a drink improperly, at least go through the motions of altering it according to his or her wishes. Sometimes a difficult customer has had a hard day, just wants a little more attention, or happens to be a complete jerk. Never say, "No, you're wrong. The recipe for a White Russian does not call for mayonnaise." Nobody ever got rich by taking the moral high ground.

Always treat customers courteously; never hurry them or show irritation. The moment a customer arrives, you should spring into action; smile, greet the guest warmly, and drop whatever you were doing to wait on him or her. Try to remember the faces (names, if introduced) and tastes of your regular customers so that you can ask them if they want "the usual" as soon as they come in. This is very clichéd, but it also happens to be appreciated in the extreme by customers. Once someone has established the rapport of a regular, tips invariably increase.

Be aware of whom you talk to and when. Never appear to be listening in on a conversation or trying to take part. As soon as you have served a drink, step back from the customer or move away. Some folks will want to talk to you... desperately. You'll quickly learn to spot those, and if you bartend long enough, you'll probably devise ingenious ways in which to avoid long conversations about their personal problems. On the other hand, a couple having a personal argument doesn't want to hear your opinion on the matter, so give them a wide berth. If invited to chat with someone for a moment, never talk about another customer or gossip about scandals you've witnessed at the bar (including your own – it's safer and more professional to leave your personal life at home).

If you must answer a telephone at the bar, do so quietly. If the call is for a patron, never say that the person is there. Instead offer to inquire, and leave it up to the customer to decide whether to answer the phone.

Customers who smoke should be indulged regardless of the medical consequences. If a customer reaches for a cigarette, light it. Replace ashtrays regularly and correctly, placing a clean ashtray over the dirty one and lifting both from the bar (to avoid scattering ashes all over the place), then place the clean tray on the table. Of course, some states and cities are now passing ordinances to prohibit smoking in bars, in which case, definitely do not light your customers' cigarettes. You can commiserate with a crestfallen smoker, decrying the jack-booted thuggery of such ordinances (although keep in mind that these laws are intended to protect bar workers from second-hand smoke), but enforce the laws on this issue.

Ultimately, you should do everything in your power to make sure that your customers are happy. Learn which customers –

both as individuals and, if you work in a bar without established regulars, as stereotypes – like to be pampered and which like to be left more or less alone when their glass is not empty. The bottom line is tips: your aim is to maximize the tips you make, and the happier the customer, the larger the tip.

DEFERENCE: "YEAH, BOSS. RIGHT AWAY, MA'AM. ANYTHING YOU SAY, SIR."

Bartenders who offend customers just lose their tips. Bartenders who offend the boss lose their jobs. Of course, one way to offend the boss is to offend the customers – but if the customer is always right, the boss is always just a little bit more right. Managers expect all bartenders, even beginners, to adhere to a set of commonsense guidelines. Therefore, if you want to keep your job, get raises, work better shifts, and earn a flattering job reference, you'd best impress the boss.

Managers and customers think highly of a busy, hard-working bartender. Even during a lull period, you can always find plenty to do around the bar: wipe spills, wash glasses, clean ashtrays, cut fruit, make pre-mixes (such as sour mix or Bloody Mary mix), and pick up glasses, straws, and napkins. Even when you talk to customers, look busy and you'll make a good impression on everybody.

Even if you don't hit that lull period, take a few seconds here and there to keep the bar clean. Customers won't want to drink at a messy, littered bar, so managers always frown upon a slob behind the bar.

If you're looking for the quickest, easiest way to get fired, try cheating on your boss. Bar managers have usually worked in the business for a long time and can tell when a bartender takes a few dollars here and there or serves free drinks to friends. In fact, managers even notice when a bartender has a heavy hand with liquor bottles. If inventories fall especially low after a certain bartender's shift, that person has poured too much into each drink.

Be stingy (within reason). Also, be thrifty regarding which brands you use. In most operations, you'll be told to put the cheapest ("house" brands) in a drink unless the customer requests a "call" or a "premium" brand (for a refresher on these terms, review Basic Bar Setup in Chapter 1).

If you want to get canned really fast, have a few drinks. Drinking on the job makes you an inefficient bartender and proves that you have no respect for the bar or the customers. All you have to do is to spill a drink, slur a few words, or insult a customer – before you can even hiccup, you'll be on the unemployment lines faster than George Costanza.

As you shower your boss with attention, don't ignore co-workers. Treat them with courtesy. Make sure to leave the bar clean, orderly, and well stocked with supplies at the end of your shift. If someone asks you to fill in for a shift, do so whenever possible. Of course, co-workers can't fire you for an unpleasant disposition, but bar work is much more fun when employees get along well and help each other.

MONEY: PASSING THE BUCKS

Proficiency in handling money requires practice. In busy bars, many errors result from giving change for the wrong amount of money, such as when a bartender mistakes a ten-dollar bill for a twenty (harder to do now that the bloated, titanic head of Andrew Jackson stares down his handlers). To minimize these errors follow the process of the "five C's": collect cash, call it, cash register, correct till-slot, and count change back.

1. Collect Cash
So you don't forget in the confusion of a busy bar, collect money for a drink right after you serve it. If your bar has a tab or check system, the manager will teach you the corrrect procedure to follow.

2. Call It

"Call" the amount of money. When the customer hands you the bill, say, "That's two-fifty out of ten." You'll be more likely to remember exactly what you have after audibly stating it.

3. Cash Register

Keep the bill on top of the cash register until you hand the customer the change. You will remember the bill that you received and will be protected if the customer insists, "But I gave you a twenty, not a ten."

4. Correct Till-Slot

Get in the habit of putting each denomination in the correct till-slot of the cash register. Then, if the customer says that you incorrectly counted the change, check the register to see if you put the bill in the wrong slot.

5. Count Change Back

Count the change back to the customer, saying, "Two-fifty out of ten: here's fifty cents for three dollars, two more to make five, and five more makes ten," as you hand back the money.

If you cannot satisfactorily handle a customer's complaint, call the manager. Usually, money complications become the manager's responsibility. Don't be insulted, however, if the manager returns the customer's money without question – remember that the customer is always right. If a similar problem occurs involving the same customer a second time, you and the manager should proceed cautiously. You're probably getting suckered.

You will also have to handle tip money in a bar. Some places pool all the tips earned in a given shift and then split the money equally among all the bartenders. This method is equitable when bartenders share areas and, therefore, customers. Never announce the amount of a tip, no matter how great or small. It's embarrassing to the customer. Not only that, it's very tacky.

DUTY: FEARLESSNESS IS FOR SUCKAS

Protect yourself and your employer. Read the section in Chapter 10 on the bartender's responsibility carefully. Given the evolution of judicial attitude toward liability, bartenders and managers are forced to assume more responsibility for the people whom they serve these days. If you do your job correctly, you will probably have to cut off a drunk from time to time. This is not much fun, but it is considerably more fun than losing a liquor license, paying a massive fine, or doing time in the Big House.

CHAPTER 10:
SIDE EFFECTS &
CONSEQUENCES

Like most other pastimes and indulgences, alcohol is best enjoyed in moderation. A glass or two of wine with dinner, hot buttered rum by the fireplace on a cold winter day, a hot dog and a beer at the ballpark – scenes like these are so idyllic that they make the pernicious world of alcohol advertisements seem almost believable. Taken at the right time and in reasonable amounts, alcohol can genuinely enhance your life.

Unfortunately, alcohol can also ruin your life. Some of the damage that alcohol wreaks on the careless and stupid is minor enough to be almost amusing. Remember the worst hangover of your life? Most people do, in vivid, graphic, horrifying detail. The average college student, for example, knows more synonyms for vomiting than does the average Eskimo for snow. A "beer gut" can also be good for a laugh especially when it belongs to someone else.

Other alcohol-related problems, however, are less easy to joke about. An overdose of alcohol can be fatal even to the healthiest person. Alcoholism – once considered the province of bums and winos – is now universally recognized as a disease that can strike people from any social or economic group. Finally, drunk drivers account for nearly half of all American traffic fatalities, and many of the victims of these accidents are innocent motorists who just happened to be in the wrong place at the wrong time.

Alcohol is a drug that can be both used and abused. Whether you plan to serve it or just drink it, you should be aware of its side effects. In this chapter, we'll discuss:

The Physiology of Alcohol
How the body metabolizes alcohol. How a person becomes drunk. How much an individual can drink before being considered drunk.

Sobering Up and the Hangover
Causes of hangovers. Modern science's unsuccessful quest for a cure.

Other Side Effects
Liquor's effect on other parts of the body besides the brain. The direct link between alcohol and unsightly weight gain.

Serious Side Effects
Alcohol abuse and the problem drinker. Drinking and driving.

Bartenders' and Hosts' Responsibilities
Legal Issues.

PHYSIOLOGY

BRAIN DRAIN

> *Always do sober what you said you'd do drunk. That will teach you to keep your mouth shut.*
> Ernest Hemingway

Your body actually produces small amounts of alcohol naturally, transforming food sugars in about 1 oz. of ethanol each day (hence the phrase "high on life..."). When it takes in additional alcohol, however, the excess is absorbed into the bloodstream and affects various parts of the body until the alcohol eventually oxidizes.

Liquor contains ethyl alcohol. The primary distinction between ethyl alcohol or ethanol and other alcohols is that ethanol metabolizes rapidly into relatively harmless substances, whereas the other alcohols metabolize slowly into poisons. It is extremely unwise to drink any type of alcohol other than ethyl. Even a small amount of isopropyl (rubbing) alcohol can cause permanent blindness, and a larger amount can be fatal.

Three basic steps take place when the body processes alcohol: absorption, distribution, and oxidation. In the absorption phase, alcohol – unlike most foods – passes rapidly into the bloodstream without being digested. Certain variables alter this process. Have you ever noticed that you get drunk faster on an empty stomach? Food keeps alcohol in the stomach longer (where absorption takes place rapidly). Bear in mind, however, that the alcohol will eventually make it to the small intestines, so gorging yourself will only delay the effects. Does champagne make you feel tipsy faster than wine? Bubbles make you get drunk faster. The carbon dioxide in any carbonated drink hastens the movement of alcohol through the stomach to the small intestine and into the bloodstream.

Body weight is also a major consideration in the attempt to gauge alcohol's effect on the drinker. Since the bloodstream distributes alcohol uniformly throughout the body, larger people – whose bloodstreams cover a lot more ground – will feel the effect of a given number of drinks less strongly than smaller people.

Once the alcohol enters the bloodstream, it passes to body organs in proportion to the amount of water they contain. The most immediate and noticeable characteristics of drunkenness occur as a result of alcohol's effect on the brain, which contains a high concentration of water. The most pronounced brain responses vary directly with the amount of alcohol measured in the bloodstream. For that reason a fairly good indication of intoxication is a measurement called the blood alcohol concentration (BAC), the percentage of alcohol in the bloodstream. (Sometimes this measurement is referred to as the BAL – the blood alcohol level.) Alcohol is a depressant, so when the BAC rises, more areas of the brain become depressed. Reactions to alcohol vary tremendously among individuals, but when the BAC reaches 0.05% in the average person, the outer layer of the brain becomes drugged and sluggish. This outer layer controls inhibitions, self-restraint, and judgment – or rather, it did when it was sober. When alcohol numbs this control center, most inhibitions fly out the proverbial window, and drinkers usually find that they have a lot more to say about everything. Given this new-found sociability and vivaciousness, people often forget that alcohol is a depressant (a frequently heard croon from the mouths of the tipsy: "How could I be so happy if it's a depressant?"). After all, any drug that leads you to call your boss a clown to his face while belching loudly enough to win a contest at the county fair must be a stimulant. Remember, however, that this feeling stems from the depression of a brain part, not the stimulation of it.

At a BAC of 0.10%, the motor area of the brain (anterior) becomes depressed and coordination becomes quite impaired. The drinker staggers, slurs words, and can't quite fit the key in the keyhole. By this point, just about all inhibitions have been drowned.

At 0.20% BAC, alcohol affects the mid-brain, the section that controls emotional behavior. At this stage, it is next to impossible for the drinker to appear sober. Sensory and motor skills have deteriorated to the point where many drinkers need to lie down. Some laugh, some cry, some become angry, some feel romantic… and some feel all these emotions at the same time, resulting in abject confusion.

A 0.30% BAC depresses the lower portion of the brain, which controls sensory perception. At this level, drinkers virtually lose consciousness; although awake, they have very little comprehension of the world around them. As the saying, goes, "The lights are on, but no one's home." This is the point at which many drinkers "black out" – after sobering up, they will have no memory of their actions. Considering the way most people with a 0.30% BAC act, this can be a mixed blessing.

Between 0.35% and 0.45% BAC, the party's over. A drinker at this level enters a coma and should be brought to a hospital. A BAC of 0.35% is generally the minimum level that causes death, so a coma is the body's defense mechanism against death. In this state, a patient will not drink anymore, so the body stands a better chance of keeping its BAC down to a survivable level.

At 0.60% BAC, the part of the brain that controls those little everyday activities, like breathing and heartbeat, becomes depressed. At this point, fatality is usually inevitable. A 0.60% BAC is actually easier to reach than you think – chugging a fifth of liquor, for example, will probably kill you in 10 minutes (Nicolas Cage's character in *Leaving Las Vegas* excepted – to reiterate: Hollywood does not depict reality).

The following list summarizes the effects of the BAC on the

brain of an average person. These responses vary, however, from person to person from day to day – see below for an explanation of other factors that affect intoxication.

BAC (%)	Effects
0.05	Release of inhibitions and self-restraint; poor judgment
0.10	Loss of coordination – staggering, slurring, clumsiness, impaired vision
0.20	Dulled sensory perception; loss of emotional control
0.30	Virtual loss of consciousness; blackout
0.35-0.45	Coma; minimum lethal level
0.60	Fatality

OTHER FACTORS

Weight/alcohol consumption data such as that shown on pg. 226 provides a handy drinking formula that allows you to figure out how drunk you will be after each drink. Do not rely on these charts, however. The only variables that they take into consideration are weight, time, number of drinks consumed, and sometimes gender (to account for different metabolisms). In the chart, one drink contains 1 oz. of 100-proof spirits, a 12 oz. beer, a 5 oz. wine, or a 3 oz. sherry. In reality, many other factors play an important role in determining degrees of intoxication.

Sleep
How much sleep did the drinker get the night before? A tired person will show the effects of alcohol more easily than an alert drinker.

Other Drugs
Did the drinker take any medication? Medicine alters alcohol's effects, sometimes drastically. Be very cautious mixing any two drugs, especially when one of them is alcohol.

Age

Younger people usually become drunk on fewer dunks. Among older drinkers, vision deteriorates more rapidly as the BAC increases.

Mood
Is the drinker in a good mood? An especially happy, sad, angry, or other mood probably will alter the person's response to alcohol.

Metabolism
How does the drinker's metabolism work? Some people oxidize alcohol faster than others. As a result, BAC can vary widely even when many other factors remain constant.

Food
Drinking on an empty stomach accelerates the rate of alcohol absorption into the bloodstream. On an empty stomach, the bloodstream can absorb alcohol in as little as two to three minutes.

Potency
The strength of the beverage can obviously speed up or stave off intoxication. If drinks are being made with more than the standard amount of liquor, the drinker will get drunk faster.

Liver Malfunction
The organ, not the food. (Sorry, that was awful....) A healthy liver plays a major role in the sobering process and thus greatly influences the degree of inebriation.

Note: One faulty assumption people often make is that beer or wine will not get them as drunk as a drink with higher-proof liquor. Wrong. A cocktail, a beer, a 5 oz. glass of wine, and a 3 oz. glass of sherry all have about the same amount of pure alcohol in them (0.6 oz.).

Relationships Among Sex, Weight, Oral Alcohol Consumption, and Blood Alcohol Levels

Blood Alcohol Levels (mg/100mL)

Alcohol (oz.)	Drinks per hour	Female 100 lbs.	Female 150 lbs.	Male 150 lbs.	Male 200 lbs.
½	1	0.045	0.03	0.025	0.019
1	2	0.09	0.06	0.05	0.037
2	4	0.18	0.12	0.10	0.07
3	6	0.27	0.18	0.15	0.11
4	8	0.36	0.24	0.20	0.15
5	10	0.45	0.30	0.25	0.18

Source: Ray, Oakley: *Drugs, Society, and Human Behavior*, 3rd ed. (St. Louis: C.V. Mosby Co., 1983). Used with permission.

SOBERING UP

Although alcohol moves quickly into the body and takes rapid effect, getting it out of the system takes a long time. Sobering up occurs through a process called oxidation, in which the liver breaks alcohol down into water and carbon dioxide. In the case of most foods, the rate of oxidation increases with activity. That is, as the body needs more energy, it breaks down the food faster. Alcohol, however, has a constant rate of oxidation that cannot be increased through exercise (making it a worthless technique when trying to sober up). For most people that rate is about 0.5 oz. of alcohol (about one drink) per hour.

In other words, sobering up is simply a matter of time. All the black coffee, brisk walks, fresh air, and cold showers in the world will not speed it up. In fact, coffee can worsen things, as it can prove volatile for a rather sensitive stomach and the last thing that you need when you're in a drunken stupor is to be in an energetic, confused stupor.

THE HANGOVER

Headache. Nausea. Stomach pains. An almost indescribable thirst. And – good lord! Who's that person on the other side of the bed??!

Hangovers can be remarkably debilitating. Drink a pint or two of tequila and chances are high that you won't spend more than half of the next day out of bed. Unless, of course, you have to go to work, in which case you'll spend more than half the day wishing that you were still in bed. While hangovers vary widely depending on a number of factors, too much of any alcohol will inevitably give you one.

Most of the agony you feel when you're hungover is caused by dehydration. Remember the 13 trips you took to the bathroom during last night's blowout? When the body processes alcohol, it uses up large amounts of water; this will not only make you very thirsty in the morning but will also produce a headache and an overall feeling of sluggishness.

The variety of additives and spices added to liquor during production and mixing comprise the second major hangover culprit. Your nausea and stomach pains can be attributed in part to a number of flavoring herbs and spices in the liquor itself; as a general rule, cheaper liquor is more likely to contain impurities and hangover-inducing, stomach-churning additives, and liqueurs are more likely than other spirits to contain herbs and spices that will upset your stomach. Certain mixers can also lead to trouble – for example, the citric acid contained in orange juice of an evening's worth of screwdrivers will probably not do your digestive system any favors (unless you consider nausea to be a gift rising up toward the heavens).

Unfortunately, there is no reliable "cure" for a hangover, despite what your Uncle Krazy Karl might be screaming from the attic. Only time – and, if possible, a long afternoon nap – will heal your self-inflicted wounds. There are, however, a few things you can do to minimize the pain.

First, drink plenty of water before bed. Drink until you're full and then drink some more. Keep a pitcher of water beside your bed in case you wake up during the night so that you can drink more. Depending on your level of drunkenness, this should counteract a great deal of the dehydration that causes hangovers. If you fell asleep before drinking water the night before, drink plenty the next morning. Resist the temptation to drink orange juice, as the acid contained therein might exacerbate your stomach pains.

Second, take a shower, sauna, or steam bath in the morning (not too long in the sauna or steam bath). Any of these will increase circulation as well as refresh and open pores, which should make you feel and look a bit less like death.

Third, take a non-aspirin pain reliever. You should avoid aspirin, which may upset your stomach. A couple of these pain relievers, especially after drinking a lot of water the night before, should reduce headache pain and other general body aches.

Even if you're really drunk and can't face the possibility of a massive hangover, avoid the temptation to empty your stomach. Although vomiting will prevent most of the alcohol left in your stomach from passing to the bloodstream and will rid your stomach of all those irritating additives, spices, and mixers, the harmful physiological side effects of induced vomiting far outweigh even the worst of hangovers. If the body decides to "clean house," you won't need to make yourself sick.

An old proverb recommends taking "a hair of the dog that bit you" (drinking more) in order to cure a hangover – logic that seems about as reasonable as the erstwhile Scottish belief that applying a few hairs of the canine that bit you would cure a wound. The person who came up with this phrase is probably long since dead; the idea certainly deserves its demise. Drinking a small amount of alcohol on a hangover will probably postpone but not eliminate the damage, but taking a restorative morning drink is a habit that's very likely to lead to alcoholism. Further, you will make your liver most unhappy if, while it's trying to rid itself of all that leftover booze, you ingest more. The dog will bite again.

OTHER SIDE EFFECTS

WEIGHT GAIN

If you're weight conscious, alcohol is the worst of both worlds – it has absolutely no nutritional value, yet it contains a large number of calories. Even worse, the mixers that you usually ingest along with most liquors tend to be very fattening as well. The calorie counts may vary depending upon the recipe, but if you're watching your weight and would like a drink, try a light beer, a glass of wine, a wine spritzer or cooler, or perhaps the pineapple-wine cooler listed in Chapter 6. If you prefer a distilled spirit, drink it either without the mixer, with soda water, or with a low-calorie mixer. Take a look at the charts on the following page.

SHORT TERM HEALTH EFFECTS

The brain isn't the only part of your body to notice the presence of alcohol. Even just one drink causes some rather harmless changes in the body; more liquor provokes more serious reactions.

The first drink or two affects the digestive system. It stimulates gastric juices in the stomach and possibly provokes a reaction in the taste buds, both of which serve to increase appetite. For this reason, people often enjoy aperitifs before meals. Aperitifs, alcoholic beverages drunk before the meal to stimulate the appetite, should be rather low in alcohol and not too warm or cold. A glass of wine, a beer, or a cocktail fits this description.

Too much alcohol might have the opposite effect – it will

stop digestion and probably deaden taste buds thus reducing appetite. On the other hand, some people eat every potato chip in sight whenever they drink too much. (It was these people – and the malicious Brits – who caused the Irish Potato Famine.) This is due more properly to the lowering of inhibitions in the brain than to any direct effect on the digestive system – when the inhibitions go, so does the diet.

Alcoholic Beverages	Amount	Calories
Beer, ale	12 oz.	about 150
Light beer	12 oz.	about 95
Distilled liquors		
80 proof	1½ oz.	97
86 proof	1½ oz.	105
94 proof	1½ oz.	116
Dry table wine	4 oz.	75-100

Mixers	Amount	Calories
Soda water	any	0
Cola	8 oz.	96
Ginger ale	8 oz.	72
Tonic water	8 oz.	72
Sour mix	4 oz.	about 50
Orange juice	8 oz.	100
Cranberry juice	8 oz.	145

Fatty Drinks	Amount	Calories
Margarita	12 oz.	375
Piña Colada	12 oz.	350
Sangría	12 oz.	250
Frozen Daiquiri	12 oz.	300
Strawberry Daiquiri	12 oz.	350
Tom Collins	12 oz.	225

When alcohol depresses the brain, many of the bodily functions that are regulated by the brain are also impaired. For instance, alcohol throws off the body's water balance, which causes the kidneys to excrete excessive amounts of water. This imbalance explains part of the dehydration problem of hangovers.

An alcohol-drugged brain also results in a lack of motor skills and sensory perception while at the same time promoting a feeling of self-confidence and sociability. This combination of effects presents a number of problems in other areas of the body. As Shakespeare noted in *Macbeth*, "It provokes the desire, but it takes away the performance." Impaired sexual performance is only one ego-deflating response of the body to a sluggish brain.

The side effects of alcohol should pose no serious threat to the moderate drinker. In fact, some studies reveal that small quantities of alcohol may even be good for you; moderate amounts of red wine, for example, have been shown to be effective in helping to prevent certain types of heart disease. At any rate, moderate and responsible drinking generally will not lead to health problems.

ALCOHOLISM

The intermediate stage between socialism and capitalism is alcoholism.
Norman Brenner

Once wrongly considered to be a weakness rather than a disease, alcoholism is still a somewhat mysterious illness. While an estimated 10.5 million people in the United State alone are alcoholics, alcoholism's causes are only partially understood. A variety of factors, both internal and external, have been linked to the development of the disease. The children of alcoholics are more likely than others to contract the disease; on the other hand, plenty of alcoholics have no family history of alcohol abuse. Certain personality traits – impulsivity, non-conformity, a sense of alienation – are shared by many alcoholics, yet it is unclear whether these are causes or merely symptoms of the disease. Emotional problems and stress can lead to substance abuse in almost any person;

alcoholics frequently use liquor to mask emotional pain or negative feelings. Social acceptability also plays a distinct role. Many college students, for example, exhibit symptoms of alcoholism that disappear once they leave the beer-soaked hallways of undergraduate life.

Whatever its causes, there are a number of symptoms that point to alcoholism:

1. Occasional "binges" – periods of uncontrolled drinking.
2. Drinking in order to get drunk or an inability to stop at just one or two drinks.
3. An increasing tolerance to alcohol – using increasingly large quantities of alcohol to achieve the same effect.
4. Work- or school-related problems that are caused by drinking; personal problems caused by drinking.
5. Avoiding family or friends while drinking; irritation at any discussion of your drinking by family or friends.
6. Failure to keep promises to yourself about controlling or cutting down your drinking.
7. Feelings of guilt about drinking; frequent regret over things you have said or done when drunk.
8. Frequent blackouts.
9. Irregular eating habits during periods of heavy drinking.
10. Using alcohol as an escape from personal problems.

This is only a partial list, but it covers most of the bases.

Number 4 is probably the most obvious symptom of alcoholism.

While its causes are unclear, the effects of alcoholism are well known. Alcohol abuse leads to a myriad of personal and professional problems: alcoholics frequently lose their jobs, friends, spouses, and children because of their inability to avoid regular heavy drinking. Suicide rates are also consistently high among alcoholics.

These emotional problems become compounded by the inevitable destruction of the chronic alcoholic's body. Physically addicted to liquor, chronic alcoholics often suffer delirium tremens (DTs) when withdrawing from alcohol without proper medical care. DTs involve three to six days of shaking, fever, acute panic, and vivid hallucinations. This experience sometimes frightens the problem drinker away from alcohol for a while, but, unfortunately, many eventually return to their previous condition.

After years of addiction, many chronic alcoholics virtually stop eating, as alcohol replaces the calories food once provided. Since alcohol has no nutritional value, most alcoholics develop serious vitamin and mineral deficiencies as well as diseases that accompany such malnutrition. Beriberi, a condition resulting from vitamin B shortages, often reveals itself in the alcoholic as Korsakoff's psychosis or Wernicke's syndrome, both characterized by gradual memory loss, confusion, and disorientation.

The liver, which plays such a large role in processing alcohol in the body, takes a tremendous beating. After just two days of heavy drinking, a person can develop fatty liver as the result of breakdown in the mechanism that moves fat from the liver into the blood. Very long periods of drinking increase the severity of this condition, or may lead to alcoholic hepatitis and inflammation of the liver. Some alcoholics' livers become scarred and hardened from abuse. This condition, known as cirrhosis, is a leading cause of death in many areas of the country.

Long-term, heavy drinking may also lead to destruction within the digestive and circulatory system. Many alcoholics develop chronic irritation of the stomach lining as the result of alcohol's constant stimulation of gastric fluids. Some contract cancer of the mouth, pharynx, larynx, or esophagus. After a long period of regularly taxing the heart, alcoholism may also give rise to heart diseases and an increased risk of high blood pressure.

Technically, alcoholism is incurable – complete abstinence allows alcoholics to lead normal lives, but most will never be able to enjoy even a social drink. Today, most rehabilitation programs revolve around detoxification. Medical professionals supervise the alcoholic's withdrawal, treat DT symptoms, provide medical care for physical ailments, and offer psychological guidance to ease the reformed alcoholic into a life of abstinence. Support groups such as Alcoholics Anonymous also help an alcoholic stay on the wagon.

DRUNK DRIVING

Simply put, driving drunk is one of the dumbest things you can do. The facts speak for themselves – over 16,000 people were killed in the United States in 1997 in alcohol-related car accidents, while over a million people were injured. Damages from drunk driving accidents and associated legal, clinical, and other expenses amount to about $45 billion per year. And if this present trend continues, there is a 60% chance that you will be involved in an alcohol-related crash at sometime in your life.

You don't need to be very drunk to cause an accident. At 0.05% BAC – only one or two drinks for some people – drivers lose inhibitions and feel more relaxed about everything. Someone at this level of intoxication might misjudge the severity of a driving situation and fail to recognize a potential accident until it's too late.

As the BAC increases, driver reflexes deteriorate. At 0.10% BAC, motor areas in the brain become depressed, resulting in slowed reaction times and uncoordinated movements. At this stage, drivers' reflexes may be too slow to respond to a hazardous situation even if they can recognize it.

At higher levels, coordination and judgment deteriorate even further. Drunk drivers also develop vision problems as alcohol affects the delicate muscle structure of the eye. With such poor powers of judgment, motor control, and eyesight, driving at this point is an invitation to tragedy.

The chart below shows the statistical relationship between BAC levels and automobile accidents. (The BAC information here and in the remainder of the section is courtesy of the Mothers Against Drunk Driving.)

BAC (%)	Risk of Accident
0.05	2-3 times normal risk
0.08	5-6 times normal risk
0.10	7-8 times normal risk
0.15	300 times normal risk

Do you remember all those drunkenness variables – mood, metabolism, age, and so on – listed earlier in the chapter? Taking those into consideration, the figures in this chart reflect the lowest probability for an individual. If a driver feels tired, is on medication, has a slow metabolism, a weak liver, or maybe just had a rough day, the chances of accident could skyrocket.

What if you do drive and happen to get caught? The consequences depend on where you are at the time. In most states, holding a driver's license gives the authorities your "implied consent" to perform a Breathalyzer test and to require that you take it. If you refuse, you face prosecution.

The Breathalyzer measures your BAC level. As of August 2005, in all 50 states, a 0.08% BAC constitutes per-se evidence of driving under the influence of alcohol – that is, conclusive evidence that you were driving drunk. This a relatively recent development that is the result of the efforts of the U.S. Department of Transportation in conjunction with organizations lie Mothers Against Drunk Driving (MADD). Previously, in many states, the VAC level for a DUI charge was 0.10%.

In addition to these laws, every state now also has laws on the books with different DUI levels for underage drinkers. This is also known as the Zero Tolerance Law. Eleven states – Alaska, Arizona, Illinois, Maine, Minnesota, North Carolina, Oklahoma, Oregon, Texas, Utah, and Wisconsin – and the District of Columbia consider drivers under 21 with a BAC above 0.00% to be driving under the influence. California and New Jersey consider drivers under 21 with a 0.01% BAC to be driving under the influence. Alabama, Arkansas, Colorado, Connecticut, Delaware, Florida, Georgia, Hawaii, Idaho, Indiana, Iowa, Kansas, Kentucky, Louisiana, Maryland, Massachusetts, Michigan, Mississippi, Missouri, Montana, Nebraska, Nevada, New Hampshire, New Mexico, New York, North Dakota, Ohio, Pennsylvania, Rhode Island, South Carolina, South Dakota, Tennessee, Vermont, Virginia, Washington, West Virginia, and Wyoming all prohibit drivers under 21 from driving with a BAC in excess of 0.02% (Hawaii has a 0.01% BAC for drivers under 18).

Don't trust these lists for too long, however; the laws are constantly being revised, usually in the direction of stricter legislation against drunk driving. For updates, you can always check out the MADD Web site: www.madd.org. Anyway, unless you go to a bar with a Breathalyzer, there's no way to measure your BAC. The safest way to protect yourself is to abstain from drinking before driving.

THE BARTENDER'S RESPONSIBILITY

All of this information affects a bartender considerably. Since judgment is the first response to fade in a drinker's dwindling brain, the bartender sometimes plays an active role in identifying customers who are too drunk to drive or to manage themselves: Perhaps concern for your customer's safety and welfare might not be enough to make your self-interested personage go through the hassle of "shutting off" a drunk. It's a lot easier to go on serving intoxicated people to keep them quiet.

If, however, someone you served gets into a drunk driving accident, the blood will fall on your hands, from both a personal and a legal point of view. Nationwide, the government and judicial systems have been cracking down on drunk driving since the 1980s. On one hand, the crackdown centers on catching and punishing people who drive under the influence of alcohol. Many states have passed stricter laws to deal with these people, including mandatory jail terms in some instances. On the other hand, legislators have recently been coming to the realization that maybe they should go closer to the root of the problem: if people don't get drunk, they won't drive drunk. After a certain point of lost judgment, however, a drinker cannot decide when to stop. Lawmakers would like to help these people by shifting the responsibility of judgment over to the people who serve liquor.

Dram shop legislation stems from this line of thought. Dram shop laws, statutes on the books of many states, make specific provisions, to prosecute the servers of drunks. If a person becomes intoxicated and causes damages, either the drunk or someone adversely affected by the drunk's actions can sue the establishment that served the liquor. It is not preserved solely for bars, either. Hosts of private parties have been held liable for damage caused by intoxicated guests.

Many states without dram shop statutes have prosecuted servers of drunks through case law. Suits against bar owners and party hosts established precedents of prosecution for similar subsequent cases.

These laws are getting tougher. In many states, the operator's license may be automatically revoked. Additionally, the bartenders themselves can be charged with a felony for intoxicating a patron. The consequences are rather drastic, since a felony can pop your ass in jail; even without hard time, a conviction on one's criminal record generally ruins the credit rating of offenders while also excluding them from such important activities as their ability to remain in their profession and their right to vote. Be forewarned.

How can you protect yourself, your patron, and the bar where you work? For starters, read this chapter carefully to learn how to recognize an intoxicated person. Some bars provide weight tables to help you decide how much to serve a person, but their accuracy is diminished by the confluence of other factors governing one's state of drunkenness, so be careful. Also remember that your bar or party may not be a drinker's first stop of the evening, further compromising the utility of these charts. Recently, some bars began to stock Breathalyzers to help patrons decide when to stop drinking and/or to call a cab. Since their use remains voluntary, however, this method has not met great success, although it's a step in the right direction. To some degree, you can shield yourself and your bar from liability by fully documenting steps that you take to prevent a drunken patron from causing harm (many bars have a journal in which you can enter relevant observations of this nature).

If a person shows signs of intoxication, do not serve that person. Then again, some drinkers slur... but they might get behind the wheel and lose control. To prevent such problems, try to keep track of your customers and don't serve anyone too much, regardless of outward appearances. Unfortunately, this is easier said than done, as many drinkers become belligerent in the face of such humiliation. To avoid unpleasant situations, be very discreet; quietly refuse to serve alcohol, then offer the guest some soda or coffee – or better yet, water. With a non-alcoholic drink, the patron probably won't feel so embarrassed about being shut off and it's very difficult for anyone to refuse the offer of a free beverage. If the customer appears to be dangerously drunk, quietly offer to call a cab. Some people will appreciate your kindness and sensitivity. Some will call you names that would normally merit washing their mouths with soap. If a patron sets off fireworks at the suggestion of a shut-off, you may have to become more forceful; summon the manager to help you and, if necessary, the police as well. Despite the hassle it might cause you at the time, your responsible, alert attitude toward intoxicated people will probably spare everybody much greater problems later.

There are other, more creative ways of dealing with drunks that some bartenders feel more comfortable employing, all of which are non-confrontational (the last thing in the world that you want to do is to provoke someone who is intoxicated). Effective server responses include first-person stories, such as stating that you're concerned about the drinker's safety, or that you could lose your job if you continue serving the patron. Offers of freebies also help – either provide a drinker with some complimentary food or a free, non-alcoholic beverage. At the very least, these actions will slow down the consumption of alcohol, and stalling can be one of the most effective and non-confrontational approaches to deal with potential problem drinkers.

Minors pose another problem. If caught serving underage people, a bar might automatically have its license suspended or revoked and be forced to pay hefty fines. Do not serve alcohol to those under 21. Ask for positive identification from all suspected underagers and refuse service if they cannot produce it. When you examine an I.D., don't just look at the birth year; also check the birth date, since it remains illegal to sell liquor to someone who is but two days shy of her magical 21st. Also check the expiration date of the I.D., and if there's some doubt about whether or not the person depicted truly owns the I.D., line up the skeletal structure of the face in a straight line going down from the forehead to the nose to the chin.

There are training courses in alcohol safety that provide a much more exhaustive outline of effective server responses and appropriate actions to undertake as a bartender. While any aspiring bartenders are well served to take such strategy course, some cities, counties, and states actually require prospective bartenders to take some kind of safety certification class. The TIPS (Training for Intervention ProcedureS) class is the most widespread of them – ask bartenders in your area if you are required to take one. Alcohol servers, after all, must experience their own ivory towers.

FOR MORE ON BARTENDING SAFETY

The TIPS program offers an excellent Web site with detailed information about state-by-state liquor (and bartending) laws, while also offering a full list of TIPS programs available in your region. Visit them at http://www.gettips.com, or contact them by 1-800-GETTIPS (1-800-438-8477). Mothers Against Drunk Driving also offers a detailed Web site that discusses laws and regulations as well as prevention and treatment measures for alcoholism and alcohol safety at http://www.madd.org. The National Highway Traffic Safety Administration explores trends and developments in laws related to drinking and serving alcohol (http://www.nhtsa.dot.gov).

CHAPTER 11: APPENDIX

Bartenders (and drinkers) love to throw around jargon to make their jobs or lives sound more interesting than they really are, but some of the following words are indispensable for communicating exactly what you want to order or mix.

TERMINOLOGY

Proof: Proof is twice the percentage of alcohol. For example, 100 proof equals 50% alcohol. This term indicates the strength of the liquor. The proof of a drink may range from 0 to 200, with most alcohols in mixed drinks being about 80 proof, the average wine around 15 proof, and the average beer running about 8 proof. These numbers are only rough guidelines; the actual proof of a liquor is usually listed on the label.

Grain Neutral Spirits (GNS): This 190-proof (95% pure) alcohol has no distinctive color, odor, or taste. Both vodka and gin are initially prepared as GNS and then later filtered or flavored and cut with distilled water. In some states it is possible to buy grain in liquor stores; if you plunge forth and purchase it, be careful! One grain drink is as intoxicating as three to four ordinary drinks, yet no flavor, color, or odor signals this potency to the drinkers. GNS is very irritating to the throat and should never be consumed straight. Everclear is the most common brand name for GNS.

Neat: Alcohol served right from the bottle with no ice.

Straight Up: A drink mixed in a glass with ice and then strained into another glass without ice (sometimes referred to as a chilled drink).

On the Rocks: Refers to a drink with ice. In some cases, the drink is prepared as a straight-up drink, but is then strained into a rocks glass with ice.

Side/Back/Chaser: Some bars, instead of regular highballs, serve a glass of mixer with 1½ oz. of liquor on the side in a shot glass. This glass of mixer is called a side, back, or chaser.

Mist/Frappé: Both terms refer to a drink served over shaved ice, but a mist is generally served in a rocks glass and a frappé in a cocktail or champagne glass. For example, a "Crème de Menthe Mist" describes crème de menthe poured over shaved ice in a rocks glass.

Dry/Sweet: Refers to the proportion of vermouth in a Martini and the kind of vermouth in a Manhattan.

Straight/Blended/Malted: These terms refer to whiskeys.

Labeling: The letters on a brandy or whiskey bottle describe the contents. They are usually listed in combination. For example, VSOP on a brandy label stands for Very Special Old Pale. These letters are primarily used in descriptive fashion, but they should give you some idea of the quality of the liquor.

C = cognac or Canadian
    E = especially
    F = fine
    M = mellow
    O = old
    P = pale
    Q = quart
    S = special or superior
    V = very
    X = extra

Virgin: A drink prepared without liquor – for example, Virgin Mary (a Bloody Mary without vodka). For a selection of non-alcoholic drinks, see Chapter 7.

Front Bar: The area of the bar in which the most frequently used liquors and mixers (vodka, gin, rum, tequila, triple sec, vermouth, Rose's Lime Juice, Scotch, bourbon, and whiskey) are held. Also known as the well or cocktail party bar.

Back Bar: Home to liqueurs, brandies, and less-frequently ordered alcohols. Also known as the liqueur bar.

House Brands: The default brands of alcohol used for making cocktails, the house brands are the ones that sit on the front bar.

Call Brands: A step up from house brands. Call brands must be ordered by name.

Premium Brands: Top-notch liquor that won't make you sicker.

Soda Gun: A force for good struggling against the evil world of bottled mixers, a soda gun allows you to dispense a variety of mixers with the mere touch of a button.

Juicers: The containers in which mixing juices are kept; they are known as store-and-pours among bartenders in the know, since their transforming tops allow them to either seal off juice from the menacing air or to pour the juice out through a nozzle.

Ethanol: Also known as ethyl alcohol, it's the stuff you can drink and from which one can procure a buzz. Its sinister siblings, methyl and isopropyl alcohol, might give you a buzz, but they might also blind or kill you in the process.

Distillation: The process of altering a substance by heating it, it is a method used to produce hard liquor.

Harvard Student Agencies Bartending Kit: An absolutely indispensable tool in becoming a masterful mixologist. Buy one today!

MEASUREMENTS

Dash/Splash: This refers to the amount of something in a drink, such as a dash of Tabasco sauce or a splash of water. Technically, a dash equals one-sixth of a teaspoon (in more precise terms, a few drops), while a splash equals a half-ounce (a long squirt), but a bartender very rarely measures these small amounts.

Shot: A shot is no precise amount. It usually ranges from 1 to 3 oz., depending on the bar and the size of its shot glasses. A shot is also a type of drink.

Jigger: 1½ oz.

Pony: 1 oz.

Nip: Nips are little bottles of liquor, popular as gifts at holiday time and as drink servings on airplanes, where they are also called miniatures. (Nips are given as gifts. People travel on airplanes around holiday season, where they serve nips. People give gifts around the holidays. Very suspicious, no?) They come in three sizes: 1, 1.6, and 2 oz.

Fifth: The traditional size of the American liquor bottle, now largely superseded by the 750 mL bottle. One-fifth of a gallon equals four-fifths of a quart or 25.6 oz.

Keg (technically, half-keg): A stainless-steel beer barrel holding 15½ gallons.

Most distillers and wine makers now use metric measurements, paying little heed to the fact that the metric system is tearing America apart. The list on the following page illustrates the relationship between standard and metric amounts.

Standard	Metric
1 pint = 16 oz.	500 mL = 16.9 oz.
1 fifth = 25.6 oz.	750 mL = 25.4 oz.
1 quart = 32 oz.	1 L = 1000 mL = 33.8 oz.

Other terms of the art in reference to bottles can get a little bit fanciful (though they are actually real, standard sizes): the Magnum (52 oz.), the Jeroboam (105 oz.), the Rehoboam (156 oz.), the Methuselah (208 oz.), the Salmanazar (312 oz.), the Balthazar (416 oz.), and finally the Nebuchadnezzar (clocking in at an amazing 520 oz. – the equivalent of 20 "normal" bottles of champagne). The last terms are seldom used, since people can't lift some of these ridiculously large bottles, let alone hoist them skyward for the purposes of pouring them. But, as an aside, a 1.5-meter-tall sherry bottle was blown in Staffordshire, England, in 1958. It holds about 26 gallons (3328 oz.) or a little over 6.5 Nebuchadnezzars. They decided to call it an Adelaide. Twenty-six gallons of wine would weigh around 220 pounds – not including all the glass, of course. You may never see or hear them again, and it can be said with some confidence that you will never witness anyone drinking them from a brown paper bag.

FOR THOSE WHO ALWAYS WANT MORE

A few Web sites have virtually mastered mixology, and those who want to find more information on that obscure drink would be well-served to consult them for those improbable bits of information that slipped through the cracks of this tome.

www.webtender.com: An outstanding site that allows you to find the recipes of a ridiculously large number of drinks. Alternatively, the site spits out a list of all known concoctions that can be produced with the ingredients of your choice.

www.TheVirtualBar.com: Virtual bar indeed… from the online jukebox to the secrets of professional bartenders to the dizzying collection of recipes down to the games, a visit to this site almost merits a line on the résumé of an aspiring bartender.

www.epicurious.com/drinking: A somewhat more nuanced approach that rounds out its drinks recipes with some fine suggestions for the use of alcohol in cooking. Thoughtful articles and an excellent dictionary of wines contribute to the sense of refinement.

www.gettips.com: An important resource for the careful bartender, this Web site details the state-by-state liquor laws and also provides information on their courses on bartending safety.

www.madd.org: Another important collection focusing on regulations and safety factors.

INDEX

Y

Z

OFFICIAL BARTENDER'S PAD
USE ONLY FOR APPLICABLE RECIPES & NOTES

_____

_____

_____

_____

_____

_____

_____

_____

_____

_____

_____

_____

_____

_____

_____

_____

_____

_____

STANDARD	METRIC
1 pint = 16 ounces (oz.)	500 milliliters (mL) = 16.9 oz.
1 fifth = 25.6 oz.	750 mL = 25.4 lz.
1 quart = 32 oz.	1 liter (L) = 33.8 oz.

OFFICIAL BARTENDER'S PAD
USE ONLY FOR APPLICABLE RECIPES & NOTES

_____

_____

_____

_____

_____

_____

_____

_____

_____

_____

_____

_____

_____

_____

_____

_____

_____

_____

_____

STANDARD	METRIC
1 pint = 16 ounces (oz.)	500 milliliters (mL) = 16.9 oz.
1 fifth = 25.6 oz.	750 mL = 25.4 lz.
1 quart = 32 oz.	1 liter (L) = 33.8 oz.

OFFICIAL BARTENDER'S PAD
USE ONLY FOR APPLICABLE RECIPES & NOTES

_____

_____

_____

_____

_____

_____

_____

_____

_____

_____

_____

_____

_____

_____

_____

_____

_____

_____

_____

_____

STANDARD	METRIC
1 pint = 16 ounces (oz.)	500 milliliters (mL) = 16.9 oz.
1 fifth = 25.6 oz.	750 mL = 25.4 lz.
1 quart = 32 oz.	1 liter (L) = 33.8 oz.

OFFICIAL BARTENDER'S PAD
USE ONLY FOR APPLICABLE RECIPES & NOTES

_____

_____

_____

_____

_____

_____

_____

_____

_____

_____

_____

_____

_____

_____

_____

_____

_____

_____

STANDARD
1 pint = 16 ounces (oz.)
1 fifth = 25.6 oz.
1 quart = 32 oz.

METRIC
500 milliliters (mL) = 16.9 oz.
750 mL = 25.4 lz.
1 liter (L) = 33.8 oz.

OFFICIAL BARTENDER'S PAD
USE ONLY FOR APPLICABLE RECIPES & NOTES

_____

_____

_____

_____

_____

_____

_____

_____

_____

_____

_____

_____

_____

_____

_____

_____

_____

_____

_____

STANDARD
1 pint = 16 ounces (oz.)
1 fifth = 25.6 oz.
1 quart = 32 oz.

METRIC
500 milliliters (mL) = 16.9 oz.
750 mL = 25.4 lz.
1 liter (L) = 33.8 oz.

OFFICIAL BARTENDER'S PAD
USE ONLY FOR APPLICABLE RECIPES & NOTES

_____

_____

_____

_____

_____

_____

_____

_____

_____

_____

_____

_____

_____

_____

_____

_____

_____

_____

_____

_____

STANDARD	METRIC
1 pint = 16 ounces (oz.)	500 milliliters (mL) = 16.9 oz.
1 fifth = 25.6 oz.	750 mL = 25.4 lz.
1 quart = 32 oz.	1 liter (L) = 33.8 oz.

OFFICIAL BARTENDER'S PAD
USE ONLY FOR APPLICABLE RECIPES & NOTES

_____

_____

_____

_____

_____

_____

_____

_____

_____

_____

_____

_____

_____

_____

_____

_____

_____

_____

_____

STANDARD	METRIC
1 pint = 16 ounces (oz.)	500 milliliters (mL) = 16.9 oz.
1 fifth = 25.6 oz.	750 mL = 25.4 lz.
1 quart = 32 oz.	1 liter (L) = 33.8 oz.

OFFICIAL BARTENDER'S PAD
USE ONLY FOR APPLICABLE RECIPES & NOTES

_____

_____

_____

_____

_____

_____

_____

_____

_____

_____

_____

_____

_____

_____

_____

_____

_____

_____

_____

_____

STANDARD	METRIC
1 pint = 16 ounces (oz.)	500 milliliters (mL) = 16.9 oz.
1 fifth = 25.6 oz.	750 mL = 25.4 lz.
1 quart = 32 oz.	1 liter (L) = 33.8 oz.

A. Bartending Kit

Comes with everything you need to be a successful bartender! Shaker, mixing glass, strainer, bar spoon, jiggy/pony, corkscrew, and six speedpourers.

$39.95

B. Extra Speedpourers

For your expanding bar needs.

$4.95

ITEM	QTY	AMT
A. Bartending Kit: $39.95 plus $5.00 postage and handling (MA residents add 5% sales tax)	____	____
B. Extra Speedpourers: $4.95 (MA residents add 5% sales tax)	____	____
TOTAL	____	____

Name: _____

Address (No. & Street): _____

City/State/Zip: _____

Telephone Number: _____

Enclose a check or money order payable to: Harvard Student Agencies, Inc., 67 Mount Auburn St., Cambridge, MA 02138, (617) 495-3033.